Taming Teenage Anxiety with CBT and DBT

A simple guide to help teens and young adults manage academic stress, build self-confidence, and make better decisions using cognitive behavioral therapy

By
LILLIAN MIDDLETON

Copyright © 2023 Lillian Middleton.

All rights reserved.

The content contained within this book may not be reproduced, duplicated, or transmitted without direct written permission from the author or the publisher. Under no circumstances will any blame or legal responsibility be held against the publisher, or author, for any damages, reparation, or monetary loss due to the information contained within this book, either directly or indirectly.

Legal Notice: This book is copyright protected. It is only for personal use. You cannot amend, distribute, sell, use, quote, or paraphrase any part, or the content within this book, without the consent of the author or publisher.

Disclaimer Notice:

Please note the information contained within this document is for educational and entertainment purposes only. All effort has been executed to present accurate, up-to date, reliable, and complete information. No warranties of any kind are declared or implied. Readers acknowledge that the author is not engaged in the rendering of legal, financial, medical, or professional advice. The content within this book has been derived from various sources. Please consult a licensed professional before attempting any techniques outlined in this book.

By reading this document, the reader agrees that under no circumstances is the author responsible for any losses, direct or indirect, that are incurred as a result of the use of the information contained within this document, including, but not limited to, errors, omissions, or inaccuracies.

IMPORTANT MESSAGE: This book is intended to provide useful information on the subject matter contained within. It is for informational and entertainment purposes only and is not intended and should not be used as a substitute for professional medical, psychological, financial, legal, or other advice, diagnosis or treatment. The author is not diagnosing conditions or offering medical or mental health advice. The information in this book is NOT intended to be used for self-diagnosis or treatment. Before you make any changes to your health routine or start any diet, you should contact your doctor. Neither the publisher nor the author shall be held liable or responsible for any loss or damage allegedly arising from any suggestion or information contained in this book. While some of the stories within are based on the experiences of actual individuals, the names and personal characteristics of individuals interviewed for this book have been altered or combined to preserve the privacy of those individuals. If you feel you require immediate help, please contact the appropriate authorities, medical providers, and/or crisis intervention service providers in your local area for immediate assistance.

Dedication

I want to dedicate this book to my long-time friend Margot. Dedicating her life to those with mental illness, she is a unicorn of a psychiatrist that offers therapy and medication management. Always there to help those in need, she generously helped me with the outline for this book, adding wisdom gained in her years of practice. I will be forever grateful for her help in making this the best book it can be so that it will be able to help the most people possible.

TABLE OF CONTENTS

Introduction xi

Chapter 1: Anxiety Is a Superpower 1
   Anxiety – How Common Is It? 2
   The Distinct Characteristics of Teen Anxiety 4
   Types of Anxiety 15
      Generalized Anxiety Disorder 15
      Social Anxiety Disorder 17
      OCD 19
      Panic Disorder 22
      Phobias 25
      Separation Anxiety Disorder 26
   Substance Use Disorders and the Anxious Teen 28

Chapter 2: Survive and Thrive 32
   Sleep and the Anxious Teenager 36
      Ways to Help Your Teen Fall Asleep and Stay Asleep . 38
   Get Your Anxious Teen Moving 43
      Yoga for Teen Anxiety 49

Yoga Breathing for Anxiety 51
Coping Skills 54
    Deep Breathing 55
    Intentional Movements... 55
    Cognitive Challenges 57
    Exposure 57
    EFT Tapping... 58
    More Coping Techniques 58
Mindfulness Meditation 60
    FAQs about Mindfulness Meditation for Teens 62
    A Simple Mindfulness Meditation for Teens 65
    More Mindfulness Practice for Daily Life...................... 67

Chapter 3: What You Eat and What's Eating You................ 70
Foods That Your Anxious Teen Should Avoid 73
    Refined sugars.. 73
    Simple carbohydrates 75
    Gluten.. 77
    Processed vegetable oils 79
    Red and processed meat... 79
    Items containing trans fats 80
Foods That Help Calm Anxiety Symptoms........................ 81
General Nutrition Recommendations for Managing Anxiety.. 84
    Avoid stimulating substances like caffeine, alcohol, and nicotine 84

Drink enough water 85

Get enough vitamin D...85

Eat foods rich in omega-3 fatty acids................................86

Include turmeric in your diet...87

Eat more fermented foods 87

Eat foods rich in zinc...88

Eat three balanced meals a day and a healthy snack every few hours 88

Eat a healthy and balanced diet like the Mediterranean diet 90

Chapter 4: She Speaks: A Teen's Anxiety Story 100

Chapter 5: CBT I: Fact or Feeling? 114

What Is Cognitive Behavioral Therapy? 114

The ABC Model and How It Works.............................117

CBT vs. Psychodynamic Therapy 121

Features of CBT 124

Emotional responsive...124

Employs understanding and rationale 125

Time-limited 125

Collaborative 126

Structured with active engagement..............................126

The Benefits of CBT 127

Expected CBT Outcomes 133

Identify Negative Thoughts...133

Practice New Skills 133
   Set Goals 134
   Problem-Solve 134
   Self-Monitor 136
CBT Techniques 136
   Journaling 136
   Nightmare exposure and rescripting 136
   Relaxed breathing 137
   Progressive muscle relaxation 137
   Deciphering cognitive distortions 137
   Playing the script until the end 138
   Cognitive restructuring 139
   Interoceptive exposure 139
   Exposure and response prevention 139
More CBT Exercises 140
   Reframing negative thoughts 140
   Worry journaling 141
   Social role-playing 141
   Mindfulness meditation 142
CBT Techniques with Worksheets 142
   Fact checking worksheet 142
   Thoughts are not facts 143
   Thought records worksheet 146
   Graded exposure worksheet 149
Potential Challenges of CBT 152

Getting Started with CBT 154

Chapter 6: CBT II: Face Your Fears 156

More about PE 158

Exposure and Response Prevention for Treatment of OCD 159

Using PE to Treat PTSD in Adolescents 161

    Imaginal exposure 162

    In vivo exposure 162

Obstacles to Exposure Treatment 164

The Need for a Multifaceted and Adaptable Plan 166

Chapter 7: DBT – Acceptance and Change 168

What Is DBT? 168

Who Needs DBT? 170

The First Four Core Skills of DBT 172

    Mindfulness 172

    Emotion Regulation 173

    Interpersonal Effectiveness 173

    Distress Tolerance 174

The Fifth Core Skill of DBT 174

Radical Acceptance 175

The Ultimate DBT Skill That Can Lift Almost Any Teen's Negative Outlook 178

Chapter 8: Continuing the Journey 180

Crisis Phone Numbers 180

Books 181
Helpful Websites 182
Anxiety Apps 183
    Breathe2Relax 183
    Calm 183
    Headspace 184

In the End 185

References 188

INTRODUCTION

One minute, you're fine. Life is good. You're functioning as you should. Your arms, legs, and mind feel like your own...

And the next, it's like every breath you take is a knife stabbing your chest. You try to control this pain, but it's hard because your mind is messing with you. It's raining on you, a thunderstorm of negative talk, saying you deserve this pain, and you're not good enough. These thoughts spiral out of control fast, building and growing into a monster that seems undefeatable. Dread squeezes your heart, and your body no longer feels like your own as you sweat and shake and fight nausea that makes you want to regurgitate your insides. All you want to do is escape, but you can't. How can you run from yourself? It feels like no one understands. They think you're just a kid looking for attention.

Almost 32% of teens in the US have an anxiety disorder. The scenario described above seems like a scene out of a horror movie, but this is the reality they face in the grips of an anxiety attack.

Anxiety is for adults, some people say. It's no big deal; others lament. It's just a phase, some insist. You'll get over it. These hurtful myths are just the tip of the iceberg. So, is it any wonder that so many teens hide their symptoms and do not get the help they need?

Anxiety is an actual illness; just like any other illness, it hurts and debilitates.

Has your teenager experienced any of the following:

- Headaches, shortness of breath, heart palpitations, stomach upset, muscle weakness, or muscle aches?

- The pain of being isolated and having no friends or other people they can relate to because social anxiety cripples their interactions with other people?

- Do they lack the confidence to pursue even the things they love?

- Is their athletic ability hampered by overwhelming performance anxiety? Or because they can't get out of their heads long enough to concentrate on the competition?

- Are your family dynamics breaking down because of your teenager's sudden anger and outbursts due to severe anxiety?

- Do you feel helpless and in pain watching your adolescent go through these things?

Most teenagers suffering from anxiety disorders are at a loss for how to alleviate their pain, especially when assistance like therapy is either too expensive or unavailable.

I was once such a teen, suffering like this and not knowing how to deal with it. I also know what it is like to be on the other side of the fence where I watch my teenage daughter struggle with Generalized Anxiety Disorder.

It seems hopeless on either side of the fence, but I can tell you confidently that there is hope. But first, I have to tell you a secret. It may be shocking. Anxiety is a superpower! Not only does it keep us safe by not making idiotic decisions, like petting that fuzzy grizzly bear, but it also allows us to see the outcomes of every decision so we can avoid catastrophe. Well, more on that in Chapter One. The point is that anxiety will always be with you or your teen, and you should see that as a good thing! The crucial struggle is to get you or your teenager's anxiety levels down to a manageable level.

I can confidently say I have done that. Name a therapy, coping skill, or relaxation exercise, and I have either done it to reclaim my mind and my life from the grips of anxiety or heard of its use. My anxiety no longer gets the best of me. I continue to use coping skills and specific therapeutic approaches to keep my anxiety at bay. And now, I am helping my teenage daughter achieve the same goal. If you are a teen with an anxiety disorder, I want to teach you the same lessons I am imparting to my daughter. I am not here to preach to you or shove scientific jargon and statistics down your throat. I want to show you how this works in the real world. Along with the strategies I will outline, I will also include stories from a teenager just like you who used these therapeutic tools to manage her anxiety and live a productive and more fulfilling life. She was eager to share her story with me to help other teenagers struggling with anxiety disorders, just like she has for years.

If you are a concerned parent of an anxious teenager, I hope that you read this book with your teen, and both see the light at the end of the tunnel and stop suffering from the pain of anxiety. This book will investigate a teenager's daily life and tweak one thing at a time to help your budding adult become the best they can be instead of having their potential clipped by an invisible monster.

The time to act is now. You can't keep waiting and hoping that one day these struggles will disappear. Anxiety affects one in three teenagers. If left untreated, their dread can morph into ideas of self-harm and suicide.

- **Did you know that suicide was "the second-leading cause of death among 10- to 24-year-olds" in 2018 in the US?**
- **Did you know that a *2019 Youth Behavioral Risk Factor Surveillance System* found that 18.8% of high school students in the US seriously contemplated suicide?**
- **While 8.9% of adolescents attempted to take their life?**

The most heartbreaking thing about these facts is that teenage suicide is preventable. It starts with education, followed up with access to resources that improve their outlook on life. This book has both these antidotes inside its pages.

First, if you are a teenager reading this book, I offer this advice before we go any further:

If you or anyone you know has thoughts of self-harming or suicide, call 911, 999, or the suicide hotline.

Just dial 988 if you are in the US to reach a listening ear on the *National Suicide and Crisis Lifeline*.

Support is always there.

Your life matters.

You are seen.

You are worthy.

The world needs you.

This book was written to be a trusted friend, a companion if you will, for the moments that you feel the most down in the dumps if you are a teen or for parents who are at their wit's end as to how to help their troubled child. It is not a replacement for therapy, medication, or medical treatment, even though I wish it could be. Anxiety can be debilitating, and it is best to consult a medical professional before it reaches a crisis level. I cannot stress this enough. Never be ashamed of seeking help or treatment. It makes you a much stronger individual to admit when you need a helping hand or even a shoulder to cry on. Tears are a purge of the messy things inside us, not a symbol of weakness for which they are mistaken.

As you continue to read, make your time on these pages meaningful to you. Open yourself up to growth. Be receptive to healing. Explore yourself so that you gain purpose as you deal with this condition.

I hope this book finds the people that need it most in time so that another teen does not become a dismal statistic. I fervently hope this book shows teenagers that they are not alone in their suffering and gives them the tools to alleviate their anxiety. I hope it helps them manage their panic so they can make friends and feel more confident. I wrote this book using my own experiences and knowledge to create a fun and engaging book for parents of teenagers (that, hopefully, their teens will read as well) to understand anxiety disorders and their treatments. I, however, did not conceive it alone. I also picked the brain of my best friend, who happens to be a psychiatrist. I share her wise and profound insights gained from years of treating patients, most of them college students, with you in the coming chapters.

Take a moment to picture this with me. Now we see a starkly different scene from the one that opened this book. The rain stops pouring inside your head, and the clouds clear to reveal the sun. It feels warm on your skin, and you lift your head to soak up the rays. You exhale, a sweet release taking away the tension you've been holding on to for so long. Your heart beats steadily in your chest. Hope makes it beat with an enthusiastic rhythm. You smile because you feel capable and loved. You feel like yourself. Your mind is your own, not hijacked by negativity. Instead, your thoughts are threads of positivity that take away the pain.

That is the goal of this book: To help one teenager at a time finally shake off the skin of anxiety to live a better life.

Turn the page to make this a reality!

CHAPTER 1

Anxiety Is a Superpower

Anxiety is an evolutionary trait. It helped our caveman ancestors survive an age of doom and peril. Even today, it helps humans stay safe with the ability to anticipate a threat. I went on vacation with my family recently. I was very anxious about us contracting both COVID-19 and monkeypox. I made everyone wear KN95 face masks, long-sleeved shirts, and pants on the flight. I also brought disinfectant wipes to wipe down all areas of the seats and more so we couldn't catch anything. My anxiety made me look a little crazy to some people, and we were hot when we arrived in Hawaii, but no one got sick. Maybe your anxiety makes you worried about carbon monoxide poisoning, so you make sure your house has detectors to save you from being poisoned. Perhaps you lock your doors even in safe neighborhoods, and when all your neighbors get robbed, you don't because your anxiety caused you to lock your doors.

No doubt your teenager has many challenges, but their anxiety is not the villain it is made out to be. Anxiety exists to help keep this adult-to-be safe and react to danger with swift decision-making. Your teenager is a real-life superhero.

However, there are instances when the strength of a superpower is too much to handle. It makes your teen isolated. This budding adult is kept from building meaningful relationships. They are afraid to shine too bright because of the spotlight's repercussions (imagined and real). Does that sound anything like your teenager?

Fortunately, there is a silver lining to this story. Your teen can learn to manage their anxiety, so it does not control them. Education and knowledge activate their anxiety's superpower. With knowledge comes power. That power is your ability to help your teenager gain control over their life rather than being fearful of the symptoms of anxiety. This chapter starts your understanding by defining anxiety and why your teen suffers from it.

Anxiety – How Common Is It?

I remember it very well. The world would feel like it was closing in on me. I was being crushed, yet the feeling came not only from the outside but also from the inside. My heart would beat too fast, and my muscles were tense, like twigs on the brink of being snapped. I would sweat, and all I wanted to do was get away. Far, far away from this sense of being trapped. So, I would pace, restless. This is what anxiety feels like; dread, fear, uneasiness . . . A concoction of terrible emotions brewing like newts, frog legs, and the skin of an alligator's back in an evil witch's potion boiling in a pot.

Everyone feels this way sometimes. Anxiety was passed down through the bloodline to all of us. So, in this way, we are all superheroes. Anxiety gives a boost of energy to get things done. It is why we feel anxious before taking a test or during an interview. The fear and dread are temporary and go away when the moment has passed. This is acute anxiety.

But what if the feelings don't go away? What if they linger? That situation is not a 'what if' for some people. The feelings stay with them. Those feelings are also not things you can push to the back of your mind and deal with later. They are intense, and they demand attention in that very moment. This is a mental health disorder called chronic anxiety.

It sounds like a harrowing existence, something confined to a script in a movie or a troubled hero in a book. But the fact is, in 2017, approximately 970 million people globally suffered from a mental or substance use disorder. Of that number, most people had an anxiety disorder. That is 4% of the population on the planet!

We often focus on the difficulties adults have with daily life when in this circumstance, but the National Institutes of Health records that almost 1 in 3 (31.9%) of all US adolescents aged 13 to 18 experienced an anxiety disorder at some point during those years of their life.

Let's break down those numbers by age group:

- 13–14: 31.4%
- 15–16: 32.1%
- 17–18: 32.3%

And by gender:

- Female: 38%
- Males: 26.1%

Those numbers are not fixed, though. They are rising! Between 2007 and 2012, the number of teens with anxiety between the ages of 13 and 18 went up by 20%. Our teens feel there is no way of getting away from these feelings . . . except to end it all. Hospital admissions for suicidal teenagers doubled over the past decade.

The Distinct Characteristics of Teen Anxiety

Anxious teens are not like anxious adults or anxious children. They are stuck somewhere in the middle, feeling pressure from both sides. Adults . . . We worry about internal things for the most part. We worry about past or childhood experiences. We fixate on physical or mental health. We worry about personal development and being the best versions of ourselves that we can be.

Kids, though . . . Their worries stem more from external factors. In other words, these things are outside of themselves. Many parents have had to chase away a bug or animal that made a kiddie cry. Many parents have had to wipe away young tears because it was too dark, or a phantom of their imagination laid in wait under their beds. Many parents have been tasked with soothing fears that something terrible will happen to Mom and Dad. Thunderstorms have universally made my kids afraid of thunder, as it has many other kids in their preteen years.

Teens, though . . . Their anxiety often stems from both worlds; the external and the internal. Their bodies are changing. They usually don't recognize themselves in the mirror. Their hormones are wreaking havoc with their mind and bodies alike. Growth spurts. Acne. Weight gain. These are some of the physical changes. Then there also exist the things we can't see, like changes in moods and perceptions. Not recognizing yourself or not having an explanation as to what is happening to you is uncomfortable, to say the least. That discomfort only increases if the teen develops faster or slower than their peers. This has a significant impact on self-confidence and self-esteem. Imagine what a 14-year-old girl would feel like being pointed at or laughed at because she has developed size C breasts while her friends have just started this journey. Alternatively, put yourself in the shoes of a girl on the other end of the spectrum. She is 18 years old and flat-chested, while her friends are all more significantly advanced in that department. She feels like an outsider.

Body image is so impactful that a teen who suffers from these feelings can develop extreme anxiety called body dysmorphic disorder (BDD). This is a form of OCD (more on that in just a bit) characterized by obsessing over perceived physical flaws, even if these only exist in their minds. For instance, if your teen has a scar, it may make them feel ugly. This leads to carrying out compulsive behavior surrounding the flaw, covering up the scar with makeup, for example, or worrying about lighting. Social media plays a role in developing that fixation with perceived imperfections. It is more than vanity. Eighty percent of people with BDD become suicidal, and 27% actually make an attempt on their life.

Teens are hypervigilant about what others might think of them and how they look. This is a normal part of growing up, but teens with anxiety are debilitated by their awareness of how they are possibly perceived. They worry that they might look stupid if called upon in class and maybe give the wrong answer. What if they aren't great at the new dance trending around school? Being incompetent in such a way feels like the end of the world. They dread the idea of doing something that makes others laugh at them. Consider the horror and embarrassment of tripping over your feet in gym class or spilling something on your shirt in the cafeteria!

And let's not even mention the worry about their academic performance... Many teens are expected to maintain perfect grades and have a mind-blowing work ethic. They are pressured to make it into the best colleges and get straight A's while still being astounding athletes in all the elite extracurriculars. The weight of those expectations — their own and other peoples', like parents, teachers, and even friends — is crushing.

These scenarios might seem trivial to adults, but if we put ourselves into the shoes of the teens we once were, we would understand that teenage anxiety is like knowing the world is ending, but everyone calls you crazy.

This is a metaphor, of course. The figure of speech describes one thing by referencing something else. I beg you to embrace metaphors to allow you to better understand the complicated concepts surrounding anxiety and, more importantly, the complex nature of your teen's feelings. We will use many metaphors throughout this book to give you this insight.

Some teens get on the rollercoaster ride that is anxiety as they enter this transitionary period into adulthood. However, some teens have been anxious for years before. Their adolescence only represents a change in the nature of their worries. Some kids fly under the radar with their anxiety symptoms, and their parents are none the wiser about their anxiety. Other kids may have been functioning well despite their worries, so parents did not understand the severity of their conditions and did nothing to alleviate these symptoms. Either way, it is possible that the child's anxiety improved and resurfaced with teenagerhood's unique pressure. In some cases, it became more severe.

No matter the situation, parents often need help identifying the signs of an anxious teen. What does this developing person look like?

Ask yourself these questions to find out:

- Does your teen feel extremely self-conscious or extremely sensitive about criticism?
- Are fears and worries about routine parts of everyday life the norm for your teen?
- Is your teen regularly irritable?
- Is withdrawal from or lack of social activity a concern?
- Does your teenager avoid difficult or new situations?
- Have chronic complaints about stomach aches or headaches become normal?
- Has there been a drop in grades or repeated refusal to attend school?
- Does your child repeatedly seek reassurance?
- Do they have trouble concentrating?
- Does your teenager have trouble sleeping?
- Is your child constantly on edge?

- Do they tire easily?
- Are they tense all the time?
- Does your child use or abuse drugs or alcohol?

Did you answer yes to at least half of these questions? Then, it is safe to assume you have a teen with anxiety on your hands. Be assured that you will get the tools to help them.

If you think your teen has chronic anxiety, it is vital to have a medical evaluation done because it might be caused by a medical condition like:

- A thyroid disorder such as hyperthyroidism or hypothyroidism
- Heart disease
- Diabetes
- A side effect of medication
- A respiratory disorder such as chronic obstructive pulmonary disease (COPD), emphysema, or asthma
- Irritable bowel syndrome (IBS)

Other possible causes of anxiety in teens include:

- Illicit drug use or withdrawal from drugs or alcohol
- High expectations and pressure to succeed
- Feeling scared and threatened by the world
- The pressures of social media

Narrowing down the cause of your teen's anxiety goes a long way in overcoming it. SCARED (Screen for Child Anxiety Related Disorders) is a simple PDF, but it is a mighty screening tool. It helps teens and their parents determine if an anxiety disorder is present, and which one is most likely. SCARED is NOT intended to diagnose, and if you get a positive response from the screening tool, you should contact your doctor or a qualified psychologist/therapist at your earliest convenience.

Lillian Middleton

Screen for Child Anxiety Related Disorders (SCARED)

Child Version - Page 1 of 2 (To be filled out by the CHILD)

Name: _____ Date: _____

Directions:
Below is a list of sentences that describe how people feel. Read each phrase and decide if it is "Not True or Hardly Ever True" or "Somewhat True or Sometimes True" or "Very True or Often True" for you. Then for each sentence, fill in one circle that corresponds to the response that seems to describe you for the last 3 months.

		0 Not True or Hardly Ever True	1 Somewhat True or Sometimes True	2 Very True or Often True
1.	When I feel frightened, it is hard for me to breathe	o	o	o
2.	I get headaches when I am at school	o	o	o
3.	I don't like to be with people I don't know well	o	o	o
4.	I get scared if I sleep away from home	o	o	o
5.	I worry about other people liking me	o	o	o
6.	When I get frightened, I feel like passing out	o	o	o
7.	I am nervous	o	o	o
8.	I follow my mother or father wherever they go	o	o	o
9.	People tell me that I look nervous	o	o	o
10.	I feel nervous with people I don't know well	o	o	o
11.	My I get stomachaches at school	o	o	o
12.	When I get frightened, I feel like I am going crazy	o	o	o
13.	I worry about sleeping alone	o	o	o
14.	I worry about being as good as other kids	o	o	o
15.	When I get frightened, I feel like things are not real	o	o	o
16.	I have nightmares about something bad happening to my parents	o	o	o
17.	I worry about going to school	o	o	o
18.	When I get frightened, my heart beats fast	o	o	o
19.	I get shaky	o	o	o
20.	I have nightmares about something bad happening to me	o	o	o

Screen for Child Anxiety Related Disorders (SCARED)

Child Version - Page 2 of 2 (To be filled out by the CHILD)

		0 Not True or Hardly Ever True	1 Somewhat True or Sometimes True	2 Very True or Often True
21.	I worry about things working out for me	o	o	o
22.	When I get frightened, I sweat a lot	o	o	o
23.	I am a worrier	o	o	o
24.	I get really frightened for no reason at all	o	o	o
25.	I am afraid to be alone in the house	o	o	o
26.	It is hard for me to talk with people I don't know well	o	o	o
27.	When I get frightened, I feel like I am choking	o	o	o
28.	People tell me that I worry too much	o	o	o
29.	I don't like to be away from my family	o	o	o
30.	I am afraid of having anxiety (or panic) attacks	o	o	o
31.	I worry that something bad might happen to my parents	o	o	o
32.	I feel shy with people I don't know well	o	o	o
33.	I worry about what is going to happen in the future	o	o	o
34.	When I get frightened, I feel like throwing up	o	o	o
35.	I worry about how well I do things	o	o	o
36.	I am scared to go to school	o	o	o
37.	I worry about things that have already happened	o	o	o
38.	When I get frightened, I feel dizzy	o	o	o
39.	I feel nervous when I am with other children or adults and I have to do something while they watch me (for example: read aloud, speak, play a game, play a sport)	o	o	o
40.	I feel nervous when I am going to parties, dances, or any place where there will be people that I don't know well	o	o	o
41.	I am shy	o	o	o

*For children ages 8 to 11, it is recommended that the clinician explain all questions, or have the child answer the questionnaire sitting with an adult in case they have any questions.

Developed by Boris Birmaher, MD, Suneeta Khetarpal, MD, Marlane Cully, MEd, David Brent, MD, and Sandra McKenzie, PhD. Western Psychiatric Institute and Clinic, University of Pgh. (10/95). Email: birmaherb@msx.upmc.edu

Lillian Middleton

Screen for Child Anxiety Related Disorders (SCARED)

Parent Version - Page 1 of 2 (To be filled out by the PARENT)

Name: _____ Date: _____

Directions:
Below is a list of statements that describe how people feel. Read each statement carefully and decide if it is "Not True or Hardly Ever True" or "Somewhat True or Sometimes True" or "Very True or Often True" for your child. Then for each statement, fill in one circle that corresponds to the response that seems to describe your child <u>for the last 3 months</u>. Please respond to all statements as well as you can, even if some do not seem to concern your child.

		0 Not True or Hardly Ever True	1 Somewhat True or Sometimes True	2 Very True or Often True
1.	When my child feels frightened, it is hard for him/her to breathe	o	o	o
2.	My child gets headaches when he/she is at school	o	o	o
3.	My child doesn't like to be with people he/she doesn't know well	o	o	o
4.	My child gets scared if he/she sleeps away from home	o	o	o
5.	My child worries about other people liking him/her	o	o	o
6.	When my child gets frightened, he/she feels like passing out	o	o	o
7.	My child is nervous	o	o	o
8.	My child follows me wherever I go	o	o	o
9.	People tell me that my child looks nervous	o	o	o
10.	My child feels nervous with people he/she doesn't know well	o	o	o
11.	My child gets stomachaches at school	o	o	o
12.	When my child gets frightened, he/she feels like he/she is going crazy	o	o	o
13.	My child worries about sleeping alone	o	o	o
14.	My child worries about being as good as other kids	o	o	o
15.	When he/she gets frightened, he/she feels like things are not real	o	o	o
16.	My child has nightmares about something bad happening to his/her parents	o	o	o
17.	My child worries about going to school	o	o	o
18.	When my child gets frightened, his/her heart beats fast	o	o	o
19.	He/she gets shaky	o	o	o
20.	My child has nightmares about something bad happening to him/her	o	o	o

Screen for Child Anxiety Related Disorders (SCARED)

Parent Version - Page 2 of 2 (To be filled out by the PARENT)

		0 Not True or Hardly Ever True	1 Somewhat True or Sometimes True	2 Very True or Often True
21.	My child worries about things working out for him/her	o	o	o
22.	When my child gets frightened, he/she sweats a lot	o	o	o
23.	My child is a worrier	o	o	o
24.	My child gets really frightened for no reason at all	o	o	o
25.	My child is afraid to be alone in the house	o	o	o
26.	It is hard for my child to talk with people he/she doesn't know well	o	o	o
27.	When my child gets frightened, he/she feels like he/she is choking	o	o	o
28.	People tell me that my child worries too much	o	o	o
29.	My child doesn't like to be away from his/her family	o	o	o
30.	My child is afraid of having anxiety (or panic) attacks	o	o	o
31.	My child worries that something bad might happen to his/her parents	o	o	o
32.	My child feels shy with people he/she doesn't know well	o	o	o
33.	My child worries about what is going to happen in the future	o	o	o
34.	When my child gets frightened, he/she feels like throwing up	o	o	o
35.	My child worries about how well he/she does things	o	o	o
36.	My child is scared to go to school	o	o	o
37.	My child worries about things that have already happened	o	o	o
38.	When my child gets frightened, he/she feels dizzy	o	o	o
39.	My child feels nervous when he/she is with other children or adults and he/she has to do something while they watch him/her (for example: read aloud, speak, play a game, play a sport)	o	o	o
40.	My child feels nervous when he/she is going to parties, dances, or any place where there will be people that he/she doesn't know well	o	o	o
41.	My child is shy	o	o	o

Developed by Boris Birmaher, MD, Suneeta Khetarpal, MD, Marlane Cully, MEd, David Brent, MD, and Sandra McKenzie, PhD. Western Psychiatric Institute and Clinic, University of Pgh. (10/95). Email: birmaherb@msx.upmc.edu

SCARED Rating Scale Scoring Aide
Use with Parent and Child Versions

Question	Panic/Somatic	Generalized Anxiety	Separation	Social	School Avoidance
1					
2					
3					
4					
5					
6					
7					
8					
9					
10					
11					
12					
13					
14					
15					
16					
17					
18					
19					
20					
21					
22					
23					
24					
25					
26					
27					
28					
29					
30					
31					
32					
33					
34					
35					
36					
37					
38					
39					
40					
41					
Total	Cutoff = 7	Cutoff = 9	Cutoff = 5	Cutoff = 8	Cutoff = 3

0 = not true or hardly true
1 = somewhat true or sometimes true
2 = very true or often true

SCORING

A total score of ≥ 25 may indicate the presence of an **Anxiety Disorder**. Scores higher than 30 are more specific.

A score of **7** for items 1, 6, 9, 12, 15, 18, 19, 22, 24, 27, 30, 34, 38 may indicate **Panic Disorder** or **Significant Somatic Symptoms**.

A score of **9** for items 5, 7, 14, 21, 23, 28, 33, 35, 37 may indicate **Generalized Anxiety Disorder**.

A score of **5** for items 4, 8, 13, 16, 20, 25, 29, 31 may indicate **Separation Anxiety Disorder**.

A score of **8** for items 3, 10, 26, 32, 39, 40, 41 may indicate **Social Anxiety Disorder**.

A score of **3** for items 2, 11, 17, 36 may indicate Significant **School Avoidance**.

Total anxiety ≥ 25

Types of Anxiety

Generalized Anxiety Disorder

As I mentioned in the introduction of this book, my daughter suffers from a type of anxiety called Generalized Anxiety Disorder (GAD). A psychologist treating my young daughter described GAD to me in this way . . . Picture yourself walking down a forest path. A snake slithers across the trail. Your survival instincts kick in full force, and your body goes into fight, flight, or freeze mode. Your heart and breathing rates quicken, and you may sweat and tremble. Anxiety levels are sky-high. This is a normal reaction to a real threat; anxiety protects you in this case. After the snake has gone and the danger is no longer present, you continue walking. You see sticks on the ground as you walk and react with a heightened sense of anxiety to every branch you see as if it were a snake. You are overcome with anxiety, and every stick is a threat. This is how people with GAD react to everyday life occurrences. Many regular events in life are seen as threats. They trigger massive amounts of anxiety.

This is what your teen feels if diagnosed with GAD—multiple and widespread sources of worry that are magnified by stress. This manifests itself in the form of hyperactivity, restlessness, and difficulty paying attention. Fatigue. Sleep disturbances. Sweating excessively. Complaints of physical discomforts like stomach aches, muscle aches, and headaches. These are all signs of GAD.

Teens diagnosed with generalized anxiety disorder show notable anxiety symptoms that impair their daily function but do not meet the criteria for diagnosis with a specific type of anxiety disorder, like social anxiety disorder. It is also the diagnosis if the teen does display symptoms that meet the requirements for a particular disorder of anxiety but also has symptoms that are exacerbated beyond the parameters of that specific disorder.

Such criteria include:

- Difficulty controlling excessive anxiety and worry.
- The presence of such symptoms on more days than not for at least 6 months.
- Impaired function because of these symptoms.

The criteria stated above must also go hand-in-hand with at least one of the following symptoms:

- Irritability.
- Problems sleeping.
- Becoming easily fatigued.
- Feeling on edge or agitated.
- Muscle tension.
- Difficulty concentrating.

Be mindful that, at times, GAD may be accidentally diagnosed as attention-deficit/hyperactivity disorder (ADHD) because they share some symptoms like difficulty concentrating and hyperactivity. The distinctions? Teens with ADHD continue to display those symptoms when they are not anxious. Some teens have a double whammy; they have ADHD and an anxiety disorder.

Social Anxiety Disorder

Social anxiety is up next on the list of anxiety disorders. It shows specific anxiety symptoms. Remember that fear of your first day of school? Imagine having it played out every time you meet someone new. You feel like you should be able to handle situations like this better by now, yet you still go back to that mental place.

Some with social anxiety might display signs like:

- Stuttering.
- Laughing or smiling too much to cover their awkwardness (which ironically makes them look even more awkward).
- Being unable to keep eye contact.
- Sweating.
- Shaking.
- Taking too long to respond because their thoughts are all messed up.
- Giving short, unclear, or unrelated answers.
- Talking in a monotone voice.
- Speaking too softly or too fast.
- Looking agitated or uncomfortable.
- Being unable to stop moving their body (fiddling, biting lips, leg tapping, blinking rapidly, etc.).

If you know this person and you come across them in public, they will avoid you and act like they didn't see you even though interaction with you might be just what they have been looking forward to. That is how powerful social anxiety can be.

But what is this type of anxiety disorder exactly? It is the lasting and excessive fear of being mocked, ashamed, or embarrassed in public or social settings. People who suffer from social anxiety disorder try to avoid situations where they might be socially scrutinized. Does your teen repeatedly voice complaints about going to school? That is a sign of social anxiety. This is avoidant behavior. The same goes for not wanting to eat in front of others or refusing to go to parties. This behavior can become so severe that the teen refuses to leave the house or even their bedroom.

Excessive preparation, such as for a class presentation, may also be a telltale sign of social anxiety. The teen is worried about making a fool of themselves in front of their classmates. They think they will give the wrong answer, say something inappropriate, or even vomit. The list of worries really can go on indefinitely.

Sometimes it is easy to pin down social anxiety as caused by a regrettable and embarrassing incident. Other times, it is not so easy to locate the cause.

Social anxiety disorder is diagnosed if the symptoms persist for at least 6 months and become routine in similar settings, like having anxiety about eating in front of strangers.

OCD

Here is a metaphor for obsessive-compulsive disorder (OCD) that I find helpful. Picture there is an alien brain-slug feeding off fear. It is in your mind, injecting worrisome thoughts constantly. One after the other, they come, making you worry endlessly. That is what the alien slug wants. It thrives on the generated anxiety. The only way to starve the parasite is to ignore the thoughts.

That is what it is like to obsess, a symptom of OCD, but that is not all. Compulsions are also a typical sign that someone suffers from OCD. Compulsions can be compared to a tiny radio antenna secretly installed in one's skull. It's tuned only to a signal from a station that broadcasts instructions like *Wash your hands, wash your hands, wash your hands* . . . Sometimes the instructions are repetitive like this. Sometimes, they're elaborate. Other times, they're paranoid. But they're not your thoughts. They're broadcast from the sinister OCD station and masquerade as your own. Even though logically you know this, it is almost impossible not to obey the instructions.

OCD is a mental disorder characterized by two things:

1. Obsessions

    These are irresistible ideas or impulses to do something. The urge persists, no matter what. You feel like you must perform the action, or the world will collapse around you. This is because these obsessions arise in response to worries or fears that you will be harmed. Or that your inaction will bring harm to others.

2. Compulsions

These are irrational urges to act on an impulse. The person might be able to resist, but this resistance causes tremendous distress. These actions are done to neutralize the threat that causes worry or fear. For example, this person might constantly rearrange furniture for fear of someone falling and injuring themselves. Excessive hand washing is likely due to fear of contracting a deadly virus.

Sometimes, OCD is characterized by both symptoms. Obsessions and compulsions may be logically connected, like hand washing to avoid illness. On the other end of the spectrum, it may be illogical. An example is repeatedly counting to 50 to prevent a loved one from having a heart attack.

These symptoms, alone or combined, can interfere with academic or social functioning. OCD sneaks up on you generally, developing in childhood. Most children develop an awareness that their obsessions and compulsions are not normal. Unfortunately, the majority of kids react by hiding their symptoms. They are embarrassed and secretive about it. They don't want to be labeled as a 'bad child.' As such, they struggle for years with these symptoms before getting a formal diagnosis.

OCD might manifest as raw, chapped hands due to compulsively washing. Perhaps it is signaled by spending prolonged periods in the bathroom. Maybe your teen does assignments and schoolwork exceedingly slowly because they are making frequent corrections or are haunted by the idea of making mistakes. Perhaps they perform repetitive or odd actions, frequently check door locks, avoid contacting specific things, or chew food a particular number of times. Your teenager might request reassurance hundreds of times daily, by asking: "What if we are late getting there?" or "Am I hot? Do I have a fever?"

OCD shares symptoms with other anxiety disorders, including panic attacks, separation anxiety, and specific phobias. As such, diagnosis can be problematic.

Diagnosis is especially difficult in cases where there are:

- Early-onset psychosis (EOP): a condition where a person loses touch with reality before 18 years old. Unlike adults, telling reality apart from imagination can be tricky for younger age groups.
- Autism spectrum disorder (ASD): is also characterized by obsessions and compulsions. The difference is that, with OCD, these are found to be intrusive and problematic, while they are preferred by those on the autism spectrum.
- Complex tic disorders: hard to distinguish from compulsions. Tic disorders are more common in boys.

Other related disorders include:

- Body dysmorphic disorder
- Hoarding disorder
- Hair pulling (trichotillomania)
- Body-Focused Repetitive Behaviors (such as hair pulling, skin picking, nail biting, nose picking, and lip or cheek biting)

Diagnosis of OCD starts with a look into the teen's family history, even though no specific genes have been isolated to show a genetic link. To get teenagers to confide the nature of their obsessions and compulsions, they must have a trusted relationship with a nonjudgmental therapist. These conversations must be regular and ongoing.

The formal diagnosis hinges on whether the obsessions and compulsions are:

1. Causing substantial distress.
2. Interfering with daily functioning, such as in academics or socialization.

Panic Disorder

You're walking down a flight of stairs, and you miss one. That mini 'heart attack' feeling you get? That is what panic disorder feels like, but the feeling does not ebb as you continue on your way. No, it stays with you all day, every day.

When that mini 'heart attack' feeling overwhelms you, it is a panic attack. It is the main attribute associated with panic disorder. These are recurring spells. They occur at least once a week and last about 20 minutes. However, not every teen with panic disorder will have panic attacks.

A teen with panic disorder experiences two types of symptoms: somatic and cognitive. The somatic symptoms are the physical representation of this condition.

The list includes:

- Tremors
- Sweating
- Heart palpitations
- Chest pain
- Dizziness
- Shortness of breath or choking

Fear is the most common cognitive symptom, which can cause the teen to cry, scream, or hyperventilate. This is quite scary to endure and frightening to witness. Those who have panic attacks quite literally think they are dying. Panic attacks can occur along with other anxiety disorders like specific phobias and OCD. The kicker is that it can also appear with certain medical conditions like asthma. A panic attack can trigger an asthma attack and vice versa. A teen might only display somatic symptoms or cognitive symptoms. Experiencing both is also common. Is it any wonder parents watching their child go through this are heartbroken and desperate for a way to resolve this?

Diagnosis is achieved by:

1. Performing a physical examination to ensure that the somatic symptoms are not caused by a physical condition.
2. Looking for a record of recurrent panic attacks.

The presence or possibility of so many other disorders can complicate the testing process. Therefore, this process can be drawn out to ensure the correct diagnosis.

Unlike OCD, which has a gradual onset, panic disorders typically occur spontaneously. However, you may notice that symptoms rear their heads in certain circumstances or environments over time. As a result, your teen will attempt to avoid those situations. Unfortunately, this avoidance can lead to the development of agoraphobia. This irrational fear of extreme proportions is centered around being in open or crowded places, leaving your own home, or being in areas that are difficult to escape. Panic arises from feelings of helplessness, shame, and entrapment. As a result, your teen might avoid going to school, friends' houses, and more. Avoidance of activities that builds a healthy teen experience severely impairs normal functioning.

The following is a metaphor for agoraphobia. Gangrene is the slow death of tissue after it has been starved of blood for too long. It spreads and spreads without discrimination unless treatment is applied. It may start in the finger but eventually infect the arm. The only solution would be to amputate the arm to stop the spread. Agoraphobia is like gangrene. One avoidance festers into another and another if the fear is not addressed. Agoraphobia can advance so severely that your teen does not want to go past the streets that serve as parameters for the neighborhood. They might not be able to endure leaving the house at all.

Phobias

You see a spider. You know it's just a spider. Nevertheless, your mind morphs the image into that of an assassin with a gun pointed straight at your head. Your heart races. Your breathing quickens. Your brain is scrambling for a way to get away from the threat. Even though you know that, in reality, it is just a little spider who might also be afraid, you are terrified, nonetheless.

That is the nature of phobias. They are fears of specific things, situations, or circumstances on steroids. The fear is intense, irrational, and persistent. The strength of the fear causes the sufferers to exhibit avoidant behavior and anxiety symptoms.

What causes phobias? We haven't quite figured that out yet. Luckily, that does not hinder getting treatment, which comes mainly in the form of exposure therapy.

Diagnosis is based on noting unmistakable, persistent fear of or anxiety about a specific situation or object that has lasted for at least 6 months.

This must be accompanied by:

- The noted situation or object almost always triggers instant fear or anxiety out of proportion to the real danger. We must account for sociocultural norms.
- Active avoidance of the situation or object.
- The development of distress significantly impairs day-to-day functioning.

Also, the fear and anxiety accompanying phobias cannot be characterized as different mental disorders like social anxiety or agoraphobia.

Phobias are specific. Common phobias include:

- Acrophobia – fear of heights
- Arachnophobia – fear of spiders
- Astraphobia – fear of thunderstorms (also called brontophobia)
- Aviophobia – fear of flying or planes
- Bacteriophobia – fear of bacteria
- Claustrophobia – fear of enclosed spaces
- Coulrophobia – fear of clowns
- Zoophobia – fear of animals

Separation Anxiety Disorder

This type of anxiety is characterized by an intense, persistent fear that separation from an attachment figure (commonly one's mother) will occur. This fear is inappropriate regarding the subject's developmental level. If separation does occur, the sufferer is preoccupied with a reunion and distressed until this happens.

To understand this anxiety disorder, think about your parents or anyone else that you love as being a security blanket. This blanket keeps you warm and brings you comfort. Every time this person leaves your side, it feels like the security blanket has been ripped away. You feel cold and alone. You feel exposed and afraid. The world is scary, and that blanket no longer protects you. The only way to take away this distress is to be reunited with this person. To be wrapped up, warm, and secure once more.

Separation anxiety occurs because the teen is not secure in the probability that they will see the attachment figure again. They fear losing this person to extreme circumstances like death, kidnapping, accident, or illness. Even sleep can seem like a threat, so the teen will want to sleep next to the attachment figure or want to be always in the same room.

Separation anxiety is a normal occurrence in babies and small children. It is rare after puberty hits. However, life changes that have a tremendous psychological impact, like changing schools, moving to a new home, or the death of a relative, friend, or pet, can trigger the development of an anxiety disorder. Scientific evidence supports that there may be a genetic predisposition to developing separation anxiety.

Watching a separation scene is painful. There are typically tears shed and pleas for the attachment figure to stay. Parents are rightly upset by these behaviors, but their anxiety only compounds the teen's fears. This turns into a vicious cycle. Therapy is necessary as a treatment for both teens and parents to get out of this tragic loop.

Separation anxiety also has somatic symptoms. This includes complaints of headaches and stomach aches.

Diagnosis depends on:

1. A history of problematic separations for at least 4 weeks.

2. Fear of separation causing significant distress or impairing function, such as an inability to participate in age-appropriate activities without the attachment figure present.

Substance Use Disorders and the Anxious Teen

Almost 50% of youngsters with mental health disorders develop a substance use disorder. Anxiety symptoms become more difficult to treat. Ignoring a teen's anxiety typically only aggravates the problems.

Chronic anxiety is uncomfortable. As with any other situation where we feel ill at ease, we look for ways to cope with or eliminate the feelings. The coping mechanism that many anxious teens (not unlike anxious adults) turn to is using recreational drugs, particularly marijuana. Dr. Jerry Bubrick, Ph.D., notes that in the short term, the reality is that such a self-medicating practice does work. "It does alleviate anxiety and stress. It numbs it. It does shut off the worry part of your brain." Long term, though, that's another story. As the anxiety persists, the teen becomes dependent on the numbing qualities of the substance. The teen craves the drug when its effects wear out. To make the pain of craving and withdrawal disappear, the teen uses more of the substance, and a vicious cycle starts. The brain sends "gotta have it, gotta have it, gotta have it" signals that are almost impossible to ignore. The result is a worsening of anxiety.

Compared to other substances, alcohol is hazardous for teens with attention deficit hyperactivity disorder (ADHD). They already struggle with impulsive behaviors. This struggle is greater with alcohol clouding their judgments. Alcohol makes them feel more energetic—like they can conquer the world with one hand tied behind their backs. So, they do riskier and more aggressive things. When coupled with depressive thoughts, this impulsiveness can lead to unchecked suicidal behavior.

Many anxious teens (again, not unlike anxious adults) rationalize their use of marijuana, excusing that it is healthier than alcohol. After all, marijuana is legal in many states now for people who are over 21 years. Vaping is all the rage lately, and the option makes it easier to smoke anywhere—on the street, at home, or school. All without parents being none the wiser.

Healthier or not, Dr. Bubrick directs kids away from using recreational drugs as a means of managing the symptoms of anxiety. Reliance on a substance to get through the day means you will use it more and more. The dependence only magnifies. "If you have a joint in your pocket all the time and you're smoking during the day to get through your day at school, that's no different from having a bottle of vodka in your desk drawer at work."

Teen brains are still developing, so using drugs or alcohol to feel better means they'll run into problems more quickly than adults. These substances affect the same parts of the brain that behavioral disorders like ADHD and oppositional defiant disorder (ODD) do. The satisfaction of soothing their symptoms is immediate, but the risk of getting hooked is greater. Substance use can make it seem like they are no longer floating in a pool of hopelessness. It can reduce irritability and help them see the silver lining in a gray cloud. It can stop the wounds inflicted by negative thoughts. Those qualities disappear quickly, too. It is no wonder a teen will repeatedly turn to those coping mechanisms. But over time, the hopelessness, irritation, negative thoughts, and anxiety symptoms will grow into monsters that seem undefeatable. The effects of those drugs and alcohol will become smaller and smaller, leading to more significant usage and dependency.

"The rule of thumb is that almost half of kids with mental health disorders, if they're not treated, will end up having a substance use disorder," explains Sarper Taskiran, MD, a child and adolescent psychiatrist at the Child Mind Institute. According to a 2016 study, two-thirds of teens who develop an addiction to alcohol or drugs also suffer from at least one mental health disorder. Teenagers can solidify addiction within the initial months of substance use.

Even if a teen is not technically dependent on substance use to tame anxiety, a one-time use can severely impact a young person's future. Even cause their life to end, given the amount of fentanyl found mixed with other drugs. The influx of fentanyl is one of the primary causes of the recent uptick in overdose deaths. Teenagers may not experience cravings or withdrawal, but heavy blows can hit their social and academic lives. Even a one-time use can undermine an already in-progress treatment of anxiety. If the teen is taking prescription medication that aids with maintaining mental wellness, even one-time use can lower its effectiveness. Dr. Taskiran notes, "Also, it's not uncommon with kids who are using substances to be non-compliant with their meds."

Simply telling your anxious teen to stay away from drugs and alcohol will not be an effective deterrent. Dr. Taskiran echoes the sentiment. "The last thing I'd say from the get-go to one of my patients is, 'Marijuana is bad for you,' because the kid has heard that from teachers, parents, TV, everywhere. So instead, what I say is, 'What is it doing for you? What are you getting out of it?'" An anxious teen relying on substance use to take away anxiety sees that substance as serving a purpose. It helps them. They might even be blind to how they are injuring themselves with the use or how their use places them at risk.

"If you're trying to take something away from a teenager, you need to replace it with something," says Dr. Taskiran. "So instead of just saying, 'Don't do that, it's bad for you,' we're trying to replace the need for substance with a coping strategy, with tools for coping without the substances." You need to replace that coping mechanism with a healthier one. The following chapters dive into discussions on therapies and healthy coping skills to ease your teen's anxiety.

CHAPTER 2

Survive and Thrive

Picture it. You are in a cozy house, and it is snowing. You must go outside and shovel the sidewalk. It snows every day, so you have the same task: go out and shovel the sidewalk. If you don't, the snow will build up. It will trap you in the house, and you can't leave, even if desired.

The snow falling is your anxiety, and shoveling the sidewalk is your task for coping with your anxiety. In real life, this task translates into self-care. The snow will build up if you don't go out and dig out the path daily. The longer you put this off, the higher the snow gets. If you don't shovel for long enough, the snow will get so high that it covers your house. You cannot see out the windows anymore. You can't see the sky anymore. All you see are the house's walls, and soon, they start to close in on you. You become hopeless. You want to get out, but it feels like there is no way. When you finally get the courage to dig yourself out, it will be much more challenging than if you had just shoveled the snow daily by taking care of yourself and tending to your mental health. This analogy works for almost any mental illness, not just anxiety.

Self-care is a popular term on social media. However, the narrative usually speaks to doing physical tasks. Self-care is more than what is on the outside. Don't get me wrong; the physical is significant. Getting your body right goes a long way in getting your mind right, whether you're a teen, adult, or child. However, caring for yourself needs to be holistic. Teenagers need to care for themselves in their entirety to ensure they don't get trapped inside the house of their minds.

As it is the most popular self-care vision, let's start with the physical tasks anxious teens should do.

Physical self-care activities include:

- Physical activity and exercise.
- Getting enough sleep.
- Eating nourishing foods.
- Hygiene practices like taking a bath and even doing feel-good tasks like a manicure.

We will discuss sleep and exercise in this chapter, while nutrition will have its own chapter next.

The mind needs TLC (tender loving care) too. This self-care is called psychological self-care.

Ways to ensure this type of care include:

- Learning new things.
- Practicing mindfulness.
- Reading.
- Doing a digital detox.

Their feelings influence your teen's mind, so emotional self-care is in order. Your teen's emotional literacy will be enhanced through such tasks so that they learn to navigate their emotions, show greater empathy, and manage stress effectively.

Some examples of emotional self-care are:

- Saying no when it is right to do so instead of taking on too much, a state that induces stress.
- Making time for reflecting on and analyzing feelings.
- Practicing self-compassion with internally directed kindness.
- Being aware of and developing emotional boundaries.

Having a supportive group of friends, family members, and teachers that your teen can turn to and trust to combat loneliness gives the teen a sense that someone understands. They will not feel alone in dealing with this issue.

Some examples of social self-care are:

- Being dependable and following through with commitments to other people.
- Asking for help when needed.
- Meeting new people.
- Spending time with like-minded and well-intentioned people, such as family and friends.

Your teen might not have a career or a job, but they do have a professional life in the form of academics. Nurturing their academic lives can help teenagers grow into self-sufficient adults, not bogged down by anxiety. These young people must learn to share their strengths and gifts with the world instead of hiding them away out of fear or worry. They must learn to set clear boundaries to facilitate that growth. They must learn to live their purpose or wander through life feeling like a lost sheep.

Teen professional self-care practices include:

- Promptly doing assignments.
- Preparing for exams as best as they can.
- Expressing their academic needs to teachers and parents.
- Eating a nourishing breakfast and lunch to get the needed physical and mental stamina required to perform well at school.

A cluttered and untidy environment causes a scattered mind. Those are not good conditions for overcoming anxiety.

Environmental self-care needs to be practiced instead with activities like:

- Decluttering, organizing, and well-maintaining home, school, and even transport spaces.
- Ensuring that clothes are clean.

Beliefs and values provide a compass for living life with purpose. These are the foundations of spiritual health.

Spiritual self-care can include:

- Meditating
- Journaling
- Spending time in nature
- Going on retreats regularly
- Praying, if inclined

Sleep and the Anxious Teenager

I'm sure you can relate to the fact that my husband and I spend an aggravating amount of time trying to get our teenager out of bed in the morning. It's not your teen's fault if they hug the covers most mornings. Puberty has caused physical changes that make it difficult for them to get some shuteye before 11 PM. Add in the demands of homework and assignments, extracurricular activities, and perhaps even a part-time job, and getting to sleep on time becomes a tall order.

Teens need between 9 to 9.5 hours of sleep every night. Therefore, the early rising time required for school leads to sleep deprivation.

Teenagers need to at least sleep 1 hour more than when they were 10 years old. Physically, they are going through growth spurts, and mentally, they are going through another phase of cognitive development. Sleep helps them go through that journey as smoothly as possible. The dangers faced otherwise include developing mental health issues like depression or a substance use disorder. A sleep-deprived teen cannot concentrate well, leading to poor grades. Lack of sleep can lead to physical accidents. An anxious teen will experience a worsening of their symptoms with sleep deprivation.

Sleep anxiety is the specific fear or stress relating to falling asleep or staying asleep. There is a strong link between sleep and anxiety, which goes both ways. Anxious teens tend to have difficulties getting enough sleep, and teens who are sleep deprived tend to be more likely to develop sleep anxiety. The relationship between anxious teens and sleep can be toxic. A surge of cortisol can make sleep hard to come by due to anxiety. The higher the cortisol levels, the harder it is to fall asleep. At the same time, not getting enough sleep also increases cortisol levels. Anxiety disorders and sleep disorders tend to go hand in hand and can both cause sleep anxiety. Nine out of ten youths with anxiety develop sleep anxiety. Sleep becomes like sand or a bird in their hands. The harder they try to keep either between their fingers, the more problematic the task becomes to achieve.

Signs that your teen might be suffering from sleep anxiety are:

- Frequent mood changes that include nervousness or irritability
- Physical tension that manifests in symptoms like headaches, clenched fists, and a tight jaw
- Fidgeting
- Wobbliness

- Changes in digestion like abdominal cramping, nausea, and loss or lack of appetite
- A marked increase in breathing rates, heart rates, or perspiration

Ways to Help Your Teen Fall Asleep and Stay Asleep

It is likely to be a hard battle but helping your teen get the sleep they need is possible. All you need is a plan of attack.

The steps to this plan are as follows:

1. **Determine the causes of your teen's anxiety, stress, and sleep disruptions**

Use your powers of observation and have frank, open discussions with your teen to allow identification of the cause of sleep problems. There are several reasons your teen might be going around in this dismal circle with anxiety and sleeping, including suffering a broken heart from a breakup, worrying about an upcoming exam, and navigating the rigors of making friends. These preoccupations can keep them up at night. They might not even realize that their worries affect them this deeply. Encourage the teen to practice regular self-examination and reflection. Journaling is an excellent tool for unpacking all those thoughts so your teen can reflect and analyze their feelings. It is a proactive approach to developing self-awareness, which paves the way for greater emotional intelligence. Creating to-do lists is also a way of removing those circling thoughts that cause worry. That thought dumping highlights the stressors in your teen's life. Neither of you might be able to get rid of these stressors, but you can create boundaries for when they can take up space in your teen's mind. A tool I learned in therapy is to set up a "worry time." This time slot is when the teen is allowed to worry about their stressors. Outside the timeframe, the teen must cultivate the discipline to let these worries pass, saved for the "worry time."

Another boundary usually enforced is silencing or turning off smartphones an hour or two before bed. As great of a tool as smartphones (and other blue light-emitting devices like laptops) can be, they can also introduce anxiety to your teen through content on social media and text messages. Your teen needs that time before bedtime to decompress away from those anxiety inducers. The blue light from these devices causes reduced melatonin, the hormone that facilitates sleep. Decreased melatonin levels can cause insomnia, disruptions in the circadian rhythm, and decreased sleep time and sleep quality. Good sleep can reduce mood swings, improve concentration, and reduce fatigue. It might be beneficial to ban technology from the teen's bedroom altogether.

2. Create structure with routines that encourage good sleep hygiene

Knowing that my daughter needs to know what events are going to happen in the future was a vital lesson I had to learn to help reduce her anxiety levels. Routines give your teen a sense of predictability. The brain loves knowing what comes next because it does not have to figure it out and, thus, develop contingency plans about possible threats or mishaps. Everything seems right in the world, even if only for that time, as certainty creates calm and reduces levels of another hormone introduced during times of stress called epinephrine. You might know it by its other name — adrenaline.

3. Encourage healthy sleep habits

Sleep is something that you allow, not force. Like drug use, staying up late may work for many teens in the short term, such as when assignments have piled up. The body's natural circadian fatigue is 2 to 4 hours after sunset. After this, many teens experience a "second wind" characterized by increased energy and focus. Teenagers (especially anxious teens prone to perfectionism and procrastination) may be very productive at this time. They feel like it "proves" they don't need an earlier bedtime. But like drug use, chronic late nights will impair long-term daily function and require more long nights until efficient functioning gets so hard that it feels impossible.

The steps to establishing a good sleep routine for an anxious teen are as follows:

Enlist the help of your teen to develop a routine

Ask your teen for their input. Doing this creates a path of least resistance and makes the young person see that you value their opinion. When you and your teen are on the same page, it is more likely that this schedule will stick.

Start with one tiny change at a time

Changes create uncertainty. Make one minor change at a time, like setting a regular family dinner time. Once that minor change has become second nature, introduce another minor change. We already know the brain does not like this, so do not create an environment rich with ambiguity.

Concentrate your efforts on the time of day with minimal structure

This lack of organization causes your teen anxiety, so deal with it first. Homework and chore-doing benefit from having scheduled times. Give your teen as little as possible to figure out on the fly at these times.

Offer your teen the tools to make it more likely that they will follow through with the routine you two developed. In the long term, this will increase their productivity.

Tips for doing so include:

1. Exercise often improves sleep quality. Incorporate physical activities as part of family routines. For example, after having dinner together, go for a walk.
2. Remove stimulants like caffeine. They are anxiety-inducing because they stimulate the brain and change how the organ works. Ensure caffeine is removed from your teen's diet by 1 PM if you can't eliminate it.
3. Involve your teen in turning their bedroom into a sanctuary. Make sure to include their preferences, such as the quality of lighting and type of decor, which will determine if the space soothes them. Additionally, this space must be solely dedicated to sleep so that the brain makes that immediate association when they enter. Ensure homework is done somewhere else, perhaps in a home office or at the kitchen table.
4. Have consistent wake and sleep times.

More tips for encouraging good sleep hygiene for anxious teens include:

Rise and shine with the sun

Sunlight helps regulate the body's biological clock and makes it easier to stick to scheduled wake and sleep times. All it takes is a small habit like eating breakfast near a sunny window to benefit from this.

Rethink schedules

Find alternative times for activities that fall close to bedtime. If the teen has a jam-packed schedule, consider paring it down.

Tie sleep to anticipated privileges

A great example of this is car privileges. Marry sleep to the activity, so the teen has the incentive to get better sleep and knows there is a consequence of sleep deprivation.

Take afternoon power naps

A 30- to 45-minute nap before dinner helps combat sleep deprivation in teens better than sleeping late. Waking up later throws off their schedule and the body's sleep cycle.

Pay attention to the summer shift

It might be tempting for your teen to alter the created sleep schedule during the summer holidays from school. While a few tweaks here and there might be of little consequence, significant changes like sleeping until noon make it challenging to return to the regular school year schedule. This behavior can put you both back at square one.

Petition for later school start times

The American Academy of Pediatrics has encouraged exploring the feasibility of starting school around 8:30 AM for middle and high schoolers. Encourage your local school board to do the same.

Sleep can still elude your anxious teen even if you do everything right. Luckily, this is not a path you or your teen has to navigate alone. In addition to using the above strategies to develop good sleep hygiene, explore treatment options and seek professional medical advice. Seeking help is likely to give you and your teen more insight into what contributes to these sleep disturbances and what is necessary to correct this.

The most important thing is getting your teen on board with these plans. Foster a connection where the teen sees how better sleep will improve their outlook and how they cope with anxiety.

Get Your Anxious Teen Moving

Science proves it—the link between physical activity and depression risk is substantial in adults—so strong that it might nullify the genetic disposition toward depression. Science also backs that the same tie holds in teens. Teens have a higher risk of developing depression and, by extension, have higher suicide rates. The thing is that teens also exercise less than adults as a group. The World Health Organization

(WHO) recommends at least 1 hour of activity that gets them sweating and breathing hard daily on top of gym class. However, this is not a frequent practice. Even if your teen does not reach this quota, some physical activity will decrease the mental health struggles associated with depression and anxiety.

A 2017 study focused on a group of 11,000 European adolescents ranging in age from 13 years to 15 years. The findings were as follows:

Only 13.6% of teens met the WHO's guideline of 60 minutes of moderate to vigorous exercise daily. The outcome? There were significantly lower rates of depression and anxiety in the exercise group compared to the group with the least amount of physical activity, which was doing the recommended exercise for three days or less over the past 14 days.

The findings also highlighted that members of sports teams got an extra boost in mental health and the benefits of their physical activity. The association was particularly robust for girls.

Elaine McMahon, a researcher on the study, cites, "Moderate activity of any kind, getting out and doing something, is associated with improvements, lower levels of depressive symptoms, lower levels of anxiety, better well-being."

But what is the link between exercise and its impact on your teen's mental well-being? The answer is that exercise affects the levels of hormones that affect your teen's mood and outlook and, thus, their ability to weather anxiety's storms.

The chief hormones, also called neurochemicals, that it impacts include:

Epinephrine and Norepinephrine

These are the hormones that initiate the human "fight-or-flight" response. They cause your heart to beat faster, your breathing to escalate, and give you a boost of power to get out of there or put up your best fight to be safe. They help you make a quick decision if you are in a dangerous situation and incite an action that is most likely to keep you safe. They are also pumping through your teen's system during an anxiety attack.

Short-term, these hormones keep you safe but prolonged release, such as in chronic anxiety, affects your entire central nervous system.

The signs of this include but are not limited to:

- Confusion
- Trouble concentrating
- Memory loss
- Sleep interruptions
- Headaches
- Diarrhea
- Tearfulness
- Changes in eating patterns
- Increased anxiety

Anxiety is a self-feeding device. Exercise decreases the levels of both these hormones by effectively using them as fuel to power the motions.

Cortisol

Cortisol has many jobs in the human body.

Its tasks include:

- Ensuring the proper glucose metabolism.
- Supporting healthy immune function.
- Helping to regulate blood pressure.
- Providing an appropriate inflammatory response.

The role it's known for is facilitating a stress response. It boosts blood sugar levels to provide bursts of energy, reduce pain responses, and improve short-term memory — all to help us survive threatening situations. Whereas this response was helpful for our ancestors to escape frequent danger, it is less relevant in today's world. Most perceived threats come from within, yet the body still responds with these bursts of elevated cortisol levels. These increased levels can help you respond to stress in the short term. For example, a teen worried about performing on an exam might gain better results than expected because the presence of cortisol helped focus his attention and improved his memory during that period. When the exam is over, cortisol returns to its normal levels.

Chronic anxiety does not provide that off switch with cortisol levels. Cortisol levels remain elevated even when there is no clear and present threat or stressor, creating more significant anxiety symptoms. Sustained levels of cortisol threaten your teen's physical and mental health.

Serious health issues that may arise from this are:

- High blood pressure
- Heart disease and stroke
- Diabetes
- Digestive disorders
- Migraines
- Immune deficiencies
- Ulcers

Just like with epinephrine and norepinephrine, exercise is an effective way of burning off excess cortisol, hence lowering anxiety levels.

Endorphins

Endorphins are known as feel-good hormones because elevated amounts of them cause pleasurable feelings. These hormones do not relate to creating anxiety symptoms but help relieve them when they are present. It is the presence of those hormones causing addictions to substances used as a coping mechanism. The brain wants the emotional high they repeatedly induce, hence the feeling of cravings. This phenomenon is not just limited to substance use but also other addictions that exist. For example, some people use food as a coping mechanism, and endorphins are released when they eat. There are healthier ways to trigger the release of endorphins so that your teen copes with anxiety better. Exercising is one of those beneficial methods.

Making time for exercise at any age is challenging, but it is a must for your anxious teen for two reasons:

1. It provides immediate stress release, blasting away anxiety, so your teen's thinking is less muddled.

2. Regular and consistent exercise sessions over time train the teen's mind and body to respond to stress more effectively.

It is easy to make the association between the physical benefits and exercise, but exercise also builds mental stamina. For example, strength training gives a sense of control and power. The standard recommendation is to push yourself to do just one more repetition of an exercise. Doing that one extra repetition takes an incredible amount of physical and mental strength. Additionally, both aerobic exercises and strength training condition the mind for clearer thinking. By putting that much focus into exercising, your teen is better able to see past whatever is troubling them. Doing something hard builds confidence to do hard things. Feeling physically strong makes us feel mentally strong.

The gym can be intimidating, but there is no hard and fast rule that exercise must occur in such a place. Your teen does not have to join a sports team to get that exercise in daily, either. Other options for getting that much-needed exercise include bike riding, walking, hiking, or yoga.

The most important thing to remember is to ensure that exercise is fun. It should not be something your teen dreads doing, or it simply becomes another trigger of anxiety. Getting your teen outdoors while exercising will enhance their ability to manage negative emotions and calm thoughts better.

Yoga for Teen Anxiety

Yoga is not just a series of poses. It is an ancient Indian practice that promotes physical, mental, and spiritual control and discipline through controlling and stilling the mind. Yoga helps the anxious teen as it contains mindful movements coupled with breathing. This sequence activates the rest-and-digest system's relaxation response by stimulating the vagus nerve and taming the fight-or-flight response. Yoga increases GABA levels. This neurotransmitter promotes the relaxation of the mind. A 12-week study followed the activity of a group who either practiced yoga or walked for 1 hour 3 times weekly. The participants who did yoga had higher increases in GABA levels. By extension, their moods and anxiety levels showed better improvement. The subjects of another study were in a cognitive behavioral therapy (CBT) intervention versus a CBT intervention with a yoga component. The two groups met weekly for two months, with one group only using CBT to manage mental health while the other coupled CBT with yoga. Both groups noted improvement in stress management and anxiety symptoms, but the relief was more remarkable for the group that did both CBT and yoga.

Specifically related to teens battling anxiety, 47 ninth- and tenth-grade students in one of Massachusetts's public high schools were the subject of a yoga-focused study. They completed self-report questionnaires that assessed their mood before and after participating in a single yoga class. They did the same before and after a single physical education (PE) class the following week. The results? Participants were less angry, depressed, and tired after each session, but the after-effects were more significant after participation in yoga compared to PE.

Anxiety is such an assault on the senses because teens get caught up in their emotions. Being mindful is like a lifeline pulling them out of the trenches of their feelings. Yoga is a mindfulness practice. It teaches your teen to objectively observe what they think and feel without judging themselves and with kindness. Mindfulness stops teens from rehashing past or future events and grounds them in the present. Doing so is possible because mindfulness practices like yoga calm the activity in the limbic system, which is the part of the brain that facilitates risk-taking behaviors driven by the primitive nature embedded within our DNA. Mindfulness also helps the prefrontal cortex make better decisions and regulate emotions.

As mentioned before, it is about giving your teen healthy alternatives to cope with anxiety. Self-medicating with substances like drugs and alcohol is destructive but healthy outlets like yoga have positive outcomes. A study surrounding teenage behavior showed that practicing yoga lowered teens' disposition for smoking cigarettes. The National Institute on Drug Abuse funded this study.

Using mindfulness techniques not only helps prevent drug and alcohol use disorders, but teenagers can also use them to help recover from an addiction. A study highlighted that mindfulness was more significant in helping people stop smoking cigarettes than the American Lung Association's *Freedom From Smoking* program.

It is evident that yoga is an effective tool that:

- Increases mental well-being in addition to promoting good physical health.

- Promotes self-regulation.

It is like a chill pill that helps your teen focus better and protects from depression and anxiety without any side effects.

Like any other activity you plan to implement into your teen's routine to help them fight anxiety, it is best to get them on board by eliciting their input. It is easier to implement if parents start mindfulness practices like yoga and meditation while kids are still young. It will be a healthy, positive habit they grow with as they mature into adults.

Yoga Breathing for Anxiety

"Space in the breath creates space in the mind for quiet and concentration," says Nicole Renée. Mindful breathing is an integral part of an effective yoga session. It calms the central nervous system, so much so that it can mean a better sleeping experience at night. Mindful breathing is so effective that even when used outside of yoga, it has a calming effect quickly. If your teen struggles with test anxiety, outbursts of anger, or trouble sleeping, yoga can help with these issues. Yoga often starts by concentrating on the way you breathe. Breathing sends a message to the brain. If it is fast and shallow, it sends a signal to the brain, saying there is danger, and hormones are released to allow for fight or flight. Anxiety also skyrockets to keep the body safe. If your breathing is slow and deep, it signals the brain that things are right in the world. It says it is okay to relax, so the same effect is felt physically.

An easy breathing exercise that your teen can practice at any time to reduce anxiety is as follows:

1. Sit in a comfortable chair. Ground your feet on the floor with heels flat to the surface. Place your hands on your thighs. Ensure your fingers are relaxed.
2. Close your eyes.
3. Inhale slowly through your nose. Allow your chest and belly to expand with the intake of air. Try counting to 5, 7, or whatever feels comfortable to keep your inhales consistent. Alternatively, you can focus on phrases like "Breathing in calm" or "Breathing in."
4. Exhale slowly through the nose or mouth. Ensure the exhalation is the same length or longer than the inhalation. Allow a more natural flow of air. Repeat the count if used or use a phrase, such as "Breathing out calm" or "Breathing out."

I call this Mountain Breathing, and I say to myself, "Up the mountain and down the mountain." It helps me to visualize a small hill or mountain and my breathing going up and down the mountain.

Repeat this for several minutes, keeping your thoughts present, by concentrating on the air movement in and out of your lungs. It's okay if you get distracted. Gently note this and bring your mind back to focusing on the movement of the breath.

I suggest doing this exercise and being an example for your teen to follow. You will also gain the same benefits. As you do it, notice how you feel. Is your body more relaxed than before you started? Is your mind calmer?

This breathing practice can be well incorporated into the following yoga pose for dispelling anxiety and depression, outlined in Amy Weintraub's book called *Yoga for Depression*. Specifically, the pose helps to calm the nervous system and rejuvenates the practitioner.

It goes like this:

1. Prop yourself up as you lie on a comfortable surface by placing a folded blanket, a bolster, or a firm cushion under your back. Ensure you are adequately supported and comfortable.

2. Add another support like a cushion under your knees with legs hip-width apart or whatever feels most comfortable.

3. Stretch your arms out with palms up.

Remain like this for a minimum of 5 minutes and breathe in and out, as explained above. Every time you inhale, picture a crown being placed on your head and say out loud or in your head, "I am." Say out loud or in your head, "Here." Every time you exhale, imagine that breath transforming and going down to your feet.

Child's pose is another excellent starter yoga pose that requires only a few easy steps:

1. Kneel and sit back on your heels. You can also sit on a block if that is more comfortable.

2. Fold your body forward until your chest and abdomen rest on your thighs and your forehead touches the ground. Stretch your arms above your head, place your arms alongside your body or place your fists under your forehead.

Laughter yoga combines voluntary laughter exercises and yoga breathing techniques to laugh stress away effectively. Seems rather silly, right? However, the benefits are astounding. I can attest to this. I used to attend laughter yoga classes in the past and only stopped because of the COVID-19 pandemic. At first, I admit, it was awkward being surrounded by strangers and forcing laughter while doing what felt like ridiculous exercises. It pushed me out of my comfort zone. I imagine this is doubly so if you suffer from social anxiety.

I, however, persisted because I could see the happiness and ease on the experienced participants' faces. I wanted that feeling for myself. So, I continued forcing the laughter while getting to know the group members. Eventually, I became comfortable with the other members, and the laughter became less and less forced. I left every meeting feeling happier and less stressed. Now I spend my summers in the Poconos. Perhaps it is time to start a laughter yoga class in our community there. With everything we have been through since the pandemic's start, laughter is a much-needed commodity. Again, I encourage you to do these exercises yourself and perhaps with your teen.

Coping Skills

The following outlined coping mechanisms are tried and true for alleviating anxiety in the moment. With practice and time, they have long-term positive effects. Before we dive into the particulars, I, all the same, must advise you that they do not replace proper treatment, and you should use them in conjunction with the advice received from a mental health professional.

Deep Breathing

This practice goes by many names, including diaphragmatic breathing, abdominal breathing, and belly breathing. Still, no matter what you call it, it entails slowly and deliberately breathing to distract yourself from stressors. The intentional movement of oxygenated air helps slow a racing heartbeat and stabilize blood pressure, in addition to slowing fast breathing. You can pair it with guided imagery (imagining calming scenes or experiences) or progressive muscle relaxation (purposefully releasing physical tension in body parts or areas one by one) to compound the effects. All three of these practices activate the rest and digest function.

Deep breathing is as easy as 1–2–3. Start by breathing normally.

Then:

1. Inhale slowly through your nose. Ensure your chest and stomach expand.
2. Exhale slowly through your mouth or nose.
3. Repeat until you feel centered and relaxed.

Intentional Movements

Yoga is a series of intentional movements. Other forms include tai chi and qigong. They are all low-impact exercises with slow movements that have soothing effects on the body and mind.

Additional characteristics that calm anxiety and promote relaxation include:

- Holding postures
- Deep breathing
- Mental concentration

Tai chi consists of slow postures and movements that look like a dance. Here is a simple tai chi movement that your teen can use to dispel stress:

1. Form loose fists with arms at your sides and stand in a neutral position with legs hip-length apart.

2. Step forward slowly with one leg. Shift your weight onto that leg and lift the opposite arm to do a slow punch.

3. Bring the forward leg back. Shift your weight to the next leg.

4. Turn the punching hand so that the palm faces upward.

5. Return to the neutral pose, then repeat the movement with the other arm and leg.

Qigong, like yoga and tai chi, is an Asian practice that has been around for thousands of years. This exercise employs posture and simple movement while involving self-massage, sound, and breathing.

You can find tons of videos on the internet outlining more complicated poses (which also applies to all the practices outlined in this book), but a simple process to get you started looks like this:

1. Starting with arms at your sides, lift your forearms. Your palms should face the sky.
2. Inhale deeply.
3. Breathe out so that you empty your lungs.
4. Lower your arms as you hold your breath.
5. Repeat the movements as many times as you need.

Cognitive Challenges

Anxiety makes it seem like the worst-case scenario is the only outcome. Cognitive challenges deliberately counter negative thoughts with positive ones, particularly during an anxiety attack. For example, your teen might think, "Mom is going to yell at me" if called, even when there is no evidence to support that negative thought. The teen needs to learn to step back mentally and think about what alternative outcomes may be. Continuing with the example, the teen can instead think, "Maybe Mom wants to talk," and focus on that instead.

Exposure

This technique involves slowly but repeatedly exposing the teen to the things that induce anxiety in a controlled and safe setting. The point is to get the teen so used to the stimulus over the long term that the fears aroused decrease. Yes, the teen will be anxious initially and want to avoid the trigger, but anxiety is reduced and perhaps eliminated in time. Exposure therapy is not a technique you should do yourself. Please seek the guidance of a therapist.

EFT Tapping

EFT is the acronym for the Emotional Freedom Technique. The technique combines exposure, cognitive therapy, and acupressure to alleviate the symptoms of anxiety and stress. It also helps shift mindset toward positivity. You can turn to a certified practitioner to facilitate EFT tapping or administer it yourself.

If you go the DIY route, a simple process for gaining the benefits is:

1. Identify the problem that needs solving. In this case, it's your teen's anxiety.

2. A setup statement must be said out loud. The teen can say, "I am anxious, but I love myself completely." Such a statement exposes the teen to anxiety but shifts their mindset to a more positive one.

3. Tap the tips of your pointer and middle fingers seven times on acupoints on your face and body. A quick Google search will give you a visual representation of these points.

4. Accompany tapping with the exposure statement.

More Coping Techniques

Everyone is different, so some coping techniques work better for some anxious teens than others. Finding the ones that soothe your teen's anxiety best is a matter of experimentation. Try new techniques and note the most effective ones. Then rely on these.

Here are 25 ideas to help you get started:

1. Write something like poetry, stories, or journaling.
2. Start a gratitude journal.
3. Read a good book.
4. Draw, paint, scribble, or doodle.
5. Watch a favorite show or movie on 'Netflix,' either alone or with friends or family.
6. Spend time with a pet.
7. Go outside for 15 minutes.
8. Take a long drive.
9. Go for a walk.
10. Do a word search or crossword puzzle.
11. Sing along or simply listen to music.
12. Dance.
13. Punch pillows.
14. Have a good cry.
15. Take a nap if tired.
16. Have a relaxing bath or shower.
17. Learn a new hobby.
18. Go shopping (Window shopping also counts).
19. Bake something.
20. Play video games.

21. Clean, rearrange, or organize your bedroom.

22. Use aromatherapy (Use candles, room sprays, lotions, etc.).

23. Practice sports.

24. Study a new language.

25. Give yourself a facial using face masks.

Have your teenager choose from the list of coping techniques to see which activity would best suit them.

Mindfulness Meditation

Breathing techniques that help alleviate anxiety are wide and varied.

Other options, excluding the ones already mentioned, include:

- 4-7-8 breathing or 4-6 breathing
- Alternate nostril breathing
- Equal breathing
- Lengthening your exhale, which is excellent during panic attacks
- Lion's breath
- Mindful breathing

Mindful breathing is the foundation of mindfulness meditation. Anxiety is equivalent to a time machine for your teenager. It either sends their thoughts to a past time where they rehearse things—how it could have been done differently or a cycle of going over the same scenarios repeatedly. Alternatively, this machine takes them to the future where they ruminate on things that have not happened but perhaps *should* happen or *could* happen or *would* happen if only ... and the thoughts spiral into imaginings that have not come to fruition. It is even possible that your teen is being driven by this time machine backward and forward in time simultaneously. What a wild ride that is and ... how exhausting. It does not end, and only mental torment exists on that ride. Your teen needs to be able to switch gears to put the time machine in park.

Happiness (and relief from anxiety) does not exist in the past or future. It exists here and in the now. Mindfulness meditation teaches your teen how to put the time machine in park and follow that up by stepping out of it to focus on what is happening presently. That is the essence of mindfulness. It is an ability anyone can develop to be fully present in each moment and be aware of where they are, what they are doing, and what they are experiencing. The ability prevents overwhelm and over-reactivity. Mindfulness meditation is the practice that encourages slowing down your thoughts and calming the mind and body to enjoy the present.

Being present, we learn to accept what is. There is no judgment about what we think or feel. We learn to observe objectively what goes on in our heads, minds, and hearts. We let go of negativity when we create that space between ourselves and anxiety. Anxious behavior becomes a habit over time. They are the go-to actions in reaction to stress, but this only magnifies the stress response, negatively impacting your teen's overall health. They get caught in cycles of reactivity to thoughts and feelings of things past and things yet to come, creating a growing ball of distress. A lack of awareness to our internal environment and the impact of external factors is what allows this ball to get bigger.

I am not proposing mindfulness as a replacement for hyperreactivity to anxious thoughts and feelings. Rather, it can be a treatment. People with past traumas, like a history of abuse, are likely to resurrect memories and emotions of that time when practicing mindfulness meditation. Overwhelm (and perhaps an exacerbation of anxiety symptoms) is likely to occur in the beginning stages. If that is the case, then it is better to work with a therapist to explore and work through those wounds.

Mindfulness meditation is not a one-size-fits-all technique.

The exact steps can vary, but two factors are common threads:

1. Deep breathing
2. Awareness of mind and body

You can start off simply by sitting in a comfortable environment for 3 to 5 minutes. In that time and space, the aim is to keep a judgment-free mindset.

FAQs about Mindfulness Meditation for Teens

This section focuses on addressing frequently asked questions many parents have when using mindfulness meditation as a treatment for their teen's anxiety. I hope you gain more insight from the answers.

What props do you need to practice mindfulness meditation?

Mindfulness meditation does not require any special tools, props, or preparations (such as essential oils, candles, or even mantras) to get started. All you need is some quiet time with your thoughts and feelings.

What effect does mindfulness meditation have on anxious teens?

Anxiety activates the amygdala, the part of the brain responsible for the human survival mechanism. This part of the brain works with another part called the frontal lobe to make decisions. These two parts are still developing their connection during the teenage years, so their communication is not fine-tuned. As such, the amygdala is easily triggered in reactive response, especially during an anxiety attack.

Your teen can learn to calm these responses through meditation, which effectively rewires the brain. Just 15 minutes of mindfulness meditation every day for at least 3 weeks makes this part of the brain less reactive.

A calmer teen is one that can focus, concentrate, and remember better. Mindfulness meditation will help your teen perform better academically and in other parts of their life. Performing better boosts self-esteem. There are also positive physical effects like reduced blood pressure, heart rate, and a more effective response of the immune system. Meditation also helps prevent sleep disturbances.

What is the goal of mindfulness meditation?

A common misconception about meditation is that it is about stopping your thoughts. Trying to stop your thoughts is a lesson in futility and only causes frustration. Your mind is always thinking, and there is nothing you can do to stop that. What you can do is gently notice your thoughts rather than become engulfed by them. Allow yourself to become an observer and note the thoughts as they pass. Remain calm and anchor yourself in the moment with your breath. Picture yourself lying calmly in a grassy field. There is a cool breeze that caresses you as it moves along. You're looking up at the sky where your thoughts are the clouds that float by. Honor them by watching as they shift and change but don't try to catch or change them. They just are, and that's okay. This is a great image to keep in your mind as you meditate.

Let's use another analogy to explain. You're riding a bike through the park. There is a lot to look at, but you can't stop to look at everything as you ride along. These sights are your thoughts. Some you can stop to admire, and others you will simply move past. But you stray along the path as you ride. To keep on moving forward, you have to bring your attention back to the path repeatedly. This is what meditation does. It brings your attention back from your thoughts. Therefore, while some thoughts will catch your attention while you meditate, other thoughts will not. Your breath is your anchor. Use it to bring yourself back from the distraction of your thoughts.

You, or your teen, may inevitably find yourselves getting carried away by thoughts motivated by fear, worry, anxiety, hope, or other emotions. It happens. Don't beat yourself up over it. Just observe the place your mind took you to without judgment and find your way back with your breathing.

A Simple Mindfulness Meditation for Teens

Starting any form of meditation can be intimidating but reassure your teen that mindfulness meditation is easy to do and does not have to take more than 5 minutes if that is their choice. Start slow and easy, perhaps with 2 minutes of meditation and working your way up to 5 and then 10 minutes. It is a great activity to do with your teen in the initial stages.

Here are the four easy steps:

1. Find a quiet space and sit comfortably. Instruct your teen to either close their eyes or look straight ahead or at their lap. Breathe in and out slowly, and pay attention to the movement of air in and out of your lungs. Keep the rhythm of your breath steady. There is no judgment at this time. Mindfulness is about pulling yourself out of your head so that you become more in tune with bodily sensations. Paying homage to each breath as it comes and goes gives this needed grounding.

2. Encourage that unity with bodily sensation by asking your teen how their body feels. Instruct them to continue breathing through the description. If your teen feels anxious in the moment, reassure them that it is just a feeling and that it will pass.

3. Carry on with supporting your teen through the practice by highlighting that they are separate from

their emotions and, thus, their anxiety. Create more separation by focusing on the breath. Have them pay attention to their chest and abdomen. Notice how they contract and expand? Notice how the air feels on their nostrils with every breath in and out?

4. Continue to breathe and stay focused on the movement. Focus on your body's sensations.

If your teen is not comfortable meditating with you, they can use a smart device to guide the way. Apps like Calm or Headspace can be sampled for free. The Cleveland Clinic has a free app called Mindful Moments as well. The device can also be used as a timer so that the youngster is not constantly monitoring the time, which makes it harder to stay focused.

Meditation is an ongoing practice. Even if you do it every day for the rest of your life, no two sessions will ever be the same. As such, there is no striving for perfection because meditation is not perfect. At times, keeping your thoughts in the here and now will be more difficult than at other times. There are times when it will seem impossible. But it is not. During such times, accept the difficulty and focus on bringing your mind back to the present when it wanders. The redirection strengthens your ability to direct your attention over time. If your mind wanders, you're not "bad at meditation" or doing it wrong. That's how brains work!! Like a bicep curl, bringing your attention back, repeatedly, will improve your meditation skills.

Your teen will most likely be skeptical about trying meditation when you initially suggest it. But even teens without anxiety can benefit from learning to shut off all the noise in the world right now and be calm. Meditation is a practice that will help them throughout their entire life. You might need to ease into the practice. You don't have to meditate every day. Even meditating 3 to 4 times weekly has tremendous benefits, so that may be the best start for your teen. With such a time frame, studies show that the brain becomes altered within 8 weeks.

More Mindfulness Practice for Daily Life

Mindfulness meditation is aimed at introducing mindfulness to your teen's life. Mindfulness is not just for those minutes when your teen sits still. It is best if mindfulness becomes part of your teen's lifestyle. As such, they can always experience the benefits. Everyday activities provide an opportunity to be more mindful.

Such activities (specific to teen life) and how mindfulness can be incorporated into them include:

Teeth brushing

This is a practice we all do, and it also serves as a great opportunity to be more mindful. As you brush your teeth, feel your feet grounded on the floor, feel the back-and-forth motion of your hand, feel the bristles of the toothbrush moving on your teeth, feel the difference as your teeth get clean . . . This is a simple activity but a task that offers an immersive experience, nonetheless.

Doing dishes

Most teens (and almost everyone, really) hate doing the dishes. But just like brushing your teeth, it can become a mindful experience. Let yourself feel the water as it fills the sink. Note the feel of the water on your skin as you submerge your hands in it. Inhale the scent of the dish soap. Look at and examine the shape and size of the bubbles. Listen to the sound of the dishes clanking against each other.

Preparing to do homework

Start this state of mindfulness by either immersing yourself in silence or turning on soothing music. Straighten your spine as you imagine a tree growing tall and strong from the ground. Move into a comfortable position where you will do your homework. Move your hands alone in the space where you will be working, such as a desk or on your lap. Bring your hand to your chest and feel the rise and fall as you inhale and exhale. Imagine inhaling peace and calm and exhaling any tension you have. Before you have even started, celebrate the effort you will put into completing the task and congratulate yourself on a job well done. You are now ready to start your homework.

Mindful dancing

With all the dance crazes taking social media and teenage lives by storm, it makes sense to make this a mindful exercise. This is not about coordination and skill. Instead, it is about embracing your body's natural rhythm. Put on your favorite song or one from your favorite genre. Close your eyes and let the strains, tones, and chords seep into your mind. Feel the beat of the music in your heart and let it pulse through your veins. Listen to your body and allow it to do what it wants to do. Feel how it naturally adapts to what you're hearing. Feel the stretch of your arms and how your neck rolls. Feel how your feet touch the floor. Dance for as long as you want and keep that focus on your moves and the music.

This chapter has focused on how your teen can rewire their mind with good sleep hygiene, mindfulness meditation, and other coping techniques. Next, we highlight a vital lifestyle practice that may be the determining factor that decides which will have dominion over your teen's day—anxiety symptoms or your teen? We will examine the role of diet in taming anxiety.

CHAPTER 3

What You Eat and What's Eating You

We often talk about how the right diet can help you physically but talk about how diet affects your brain is not as common. However, to defeat anxiety, this is a subject that needs the spotlight shone upon it. Diet affects emotions and mood because of the close relationship between the brain and the gastrointestinal tract. This connection is so strong that the gastrointestinal tract is often referred to as the "second brain."

But how is this possible? We don't often link thinking and reasoning to what goes on in our guts. We should. The gastrointestinal tract is home to over a trillion bacteria. Before you cringe, you should know that most of these are "good" bacteria. They are necessary for good physical and mental health. Eating healthy food promotes the growth of these types of microorganisms, which sequentially leads to the production of neurotransmitters like dopamine and serotonin. Dopamine makes us feel pleasure and motivates us. Serotonin is a mood stabilizer. The production of higher levels of these chemical substances sets your teen up to have a happier outlook, improved focus, and fewer mood fluctuations.

On the other hand, a regular diet of junk food upsets the balance of good and bad bacteria in the gut. Fewer good bacteria are produced and, thus, the levels of these feel-good neurotransmitters plummet. When these levels are high, your brain gets the message that the world is an overall happier place, and emotions reflect that positive message. Flipping the coin, when these levels are low, it is easy to adopt a negative attitude and outlook. It is easier for anxiety symptoms to manifest.

Sugar is a particularly nasty culprit that promotes the growth of bad bacteria in the gastrointestinal tract. It leads to inflammation, something that these bacteria feed on. Chronic inflammation is linked to almost every single neurological and neurodegenerative disorder, and anxiety is on that list. Certain foods promote inflammation. Unfortunately, that list is quite extensive and generally includes foods containing refined sugars and processed vegetable oils. Foods that are high in refined sugar don't typically expose themselves for what they are. They hide with more "refined" names like cane sugar, brown sugar, syrup, fruit juice concentrate, corn sweetener, and malt sugar. Also, a red flag is any item on a food's ingredient list that ends in "-ose," such as fructose, dextrose, and sucrose. It is startling to highlight that fructose now comprises 10% of caloric intake in the United States. Such refined sugars lead to the production of AGEs (advanced glycation end products). AGEs accumulate in the body and lead to neuroinflammation, in addition to contributing to metabolic diseases like diabetes. These compounds are formed when proteins or fats combine with sugars in a process known as glycation. Corn oil and soybean oil are common names you will come across that represent the presence of processed vegetable oils in food. A particular omega-6 fatty acid called linoleic acid is found in such products. Like sugar, it causes inflammation. Not only does this initiate inflammation, but there are also a host of other negative physical implications, like an increased risk of developing cardiovascular diseases.

Inflammation is being made to seem like the bad guy here, but it is not. Inflammation is another word for swelling. This action is just one mechanism that the body uses to defend and heal itself from injuries and infections. The site of inflammation is red, puffed up, and hot because the body increases blood flow to that area. White blood cells and the other microscopic soldiers go to work protecting that area and building a defense to prevent further injury or infection.

Like anxiety, a tool meant to protect us can start to cause more damage than it does good when we don't have an internal off switch. Even when there is no threat, the mechanism is activated, and the action meant to help, now destroys the body and the mind. When this lasts for prolonged periods, ranging from months to years, it is called chronic inflammation. Acute inflammation is activated for a specific purpose and goes away once the threat has been nullified.

It is easy to identify inflammation as a problem when it goes into this overactive state when you can see it, let's say, on your arm or leg. But you can't see inflammation when it occurs inside your body, and this is when it is most problematic. It damages arteries, joints, and organs. It also impairs cognitive functions with symptoms like confusion, memory lapses, lack of motivation, fatigue, and the development of depression or anxiety.

Foods That Your Anxious Teen Should Avoid

Chronic inflammation is not something that you have to just deal with. It can be controlled and often reversed with lifestyle changes like exercising and managing stress. Taking on an anti-inflammatory diet is one of the best moves you can make to guide this immune response in a way that helps your teen be healthy in a holistic way. Let's start with the elimination aspect of an anti-inflammatory diet before highlighting items that should be included in your teen's diet. If the following items cannot be entirely removed from your teen's diet, ensure the quantity consumed is drastically reduced.

Refined sugars

More people are realizing the dangers of consuming too much sugar. The American Heart Association recommends that men consume less than 150 calories (which is about 9 teaspoons) of sugar daily. The amount for women is lower at 100 calories of sugar per day. This totals about 6 teaspoons worth of sugar. The recommended consumption for teens and kids is even lower.

Deliberate action that leads to limited sugar consumption is to check the sugar content on food labels. However, it is not only the sweet stuff like chocolate chip cookies and cakes that you must look out for. Surprisingly, items like many savory foods also contain high amounts of sugar. Take, for example, store-bought tomato basil sauce. A half-cup serving contains 12 grams of sugar. Four grams of sugar is 1 teaspoon of sugar. This half-cup serving feeds a person 3 teaspoons of sugar. Let's be honest here. Hardly anyone consumes just half a cup at mealtime. And this does not account for other items that will be served with a meal that may also contain quantities of sugar.

Food labels in the US use grams as the unit of measurement. As such, many people are unaware of how many teaspoons of sugar they consume throughout the day. The same goes for recipes that use ounces, pounds, and other units of measurement. One and a half cups of pasta sauce can seem harmless in a recipe, but this equals 36 grams of sugar. This is 9 teaspoons of sugar. This already surpasses the recommendation that men should consume daily and sets up women to do the same, as this is only one serving of food. This is too much for teens and kids.

More examples of food and drinks that contain hidden sugar include:

- Granola
- Protein bars
- Instant oatmeal
- Salad dressings
- Breakfast cereals
- Packaged fruits
- Coleslaw
- Ketchup
- Barbecue sauce
- Low-fat yogurt
- Canned fruit
- Chocolate milk
- Premade smoothies
- Energy drinks

Most of us enjoy our tea and coffee with a sweetener. Artificial sweeteners have been praised as the go-to for pleasing your palate in a safer manner. However, studies show that artificial sweeteners precipitate anxiety in animals and, in humans, the prognosis is even worse. Artificial sweeteners are linked to the development of neuropsychiatric issues, one of which includes anxiety. People who already suffer from such mental disorders are particularly susceptible to the worsening of these symptoms.

The outlook on sugar consumption is not looking great, I admit. However, sugar is not something that needs to be removed entirely from your teen's (or anyone else's) diet. Ideally, it should not be. The body needs a healthy balance of sugar and other nutritional items, such as fat and protein, to function at its best. The brain needs this balance to combat anxiety.

Therefore, instead of elimination, look to finding a healthy medium. Significantly reduce artificial sugar intake and consume sugar through natural sources. For example, eat more fresh fruit instead of consuming dried fruit or drinking fruit juice. The concentrated sugars in these products affect the body and brain differently . . . and not in a good way. Similarly, instead of using artificial sweeteners in beverages such as tea, use items such as stevia, which is a natural non-calorie sweetener, or erythritol, which is a sugar alcohol that helps tame the growth of bacteria in the gut.

Simple carbohydrates

Simple carbohydrates are broken down quickly by the body because of their structure. They are turned into sugar, which causes a spike in blood sugar levels. The pancreas produces large quantities of insulin because of this, and an inflammatory response is incited as a result. Highly processed foods and foods made with refined flour tend to be simple carbs.

Examples include:

- Pancakes
- Waffles
- Biscuits
- Flour tortillas
- Fruit juices
- Cereals containing added sugar
- White pasta, bread, and rice

Some natural items like rice and white potatoes also have the makeup of simple carbohydrates, and they should be consumed in lesser quantities.

The simple solution to avoiding inflammation incited this way is to eat more unprocessed or "whole" carbohydrates. They are broken down by the body less quickly and, therefore, do not cause a sharp increase in insulin production. Less production equates to less of an inflammatory response. An even better solution is to pair carbohydrates with a source of protein and a little bit of fat. This practice prevents a spike in insulin levels. Fiber-rich foods are examples of complex carbohydrates.

More examples of foods containing complex carbohydrates include:

- Whole wheat flour
- Brown rice
- Flaxseed
- Dried beans
- Sweet potatoes
- Nuts

- Non-starchy vegetables like zucchini, cucumbers, onions, peppers, broccoli, and cabbage

- Unsweetened cereals

Gluten

The word *gluten* has been a trending topic on various media sources throughout the last few years, but what is gluten exactly? Simply put, gluten is a protein in many cereal grains (like barley, rye, and wheat). It is responsible for the elastic texture when these grains are produced into a dough.

Most of us consume gluten in the form of bread, cereals, cakes, and pies—to name a few. Some people have an intolerance or sensitivity to gluten, known as Celiac Disease. If you are afflicted, eating gluten increases the permeability of the intestines, leading to a condition known as leaky gut. This is an overreaction of the immune system that damages the lining of the small intestine. Leaky gut is a precursor to inflammation and, therefore, anxiety. Celiac disease is often associated with panic disorders, social phobias, and other types of anxiety. At this time, research has only proven that a gluten-free diet will reduce anxiety in people with Celiac Disease. Nevertheless, I feel it is reasonable to include it in the warehouse of anxiety treatments.

Practicing a gluten-free diet is relatively simple in concept, but there are often gluten-containing foods, like soy sauce, which may come as a surprise to you.

Many foods are naturally free of gluten, including:

- Rice, including wild rice
- Lentils
- Fruits
- Vegetables
- Fish and seafood
- Lean, non-processed meats and poultry
- Potatoes

Elimination of several starches, flours, and grains is part of a gluten-free diet. However, you do not have to give up some of the items you enjoy most, like bread. You simply must get creative and be open to new flavors and textures. For example, instead of eating wheat bread or white bread, try bread made from buckwheat, which is gluten-free flour.

Other great gluten-free substitutions include:

- Gluten-free flours such as almond flour, cassava flour, coconut flour, and rice flour
- Millet
- Flax
- Arrowroot
- Buckwheat
- Teff
- Quinoa

- Tapioca
- Soy
- Amaranth
- Corn in the form of grits, polenta, and cornmeal

Processed vegetable oils

On the human evolutionary scale, processed vegetable cooking oil has not been around that long. The invention only came around in the early 1900s. Highly processed vegetable oils that quickly come to mind are canola, soy, corn, and sunflower. They were developed to be a healthy alternative to saturated animal fats, which had been used for cooking before that time. Because they are made from plant-based products, they are often referred to as "seed oils." However, specific fatty acids — omega-6 fatty acids — in such processed oils lead to inflammation.

Just like with sugar, balance is key. Opt to use less processed cooking oils such as avocado, olive, and coconut oil for sauteing, frying, and grilling your dishes.

Red and processed meat

Red meat is any meat that comes from goats, cows, pigs, and sheep. These meats are often fermented, cured, smoked, or salted to preserve and add flavor.

Therefore, you might find them in processed forms like in:

- Hot dogs
- Pepperoni
- Salami
- Bacon
- Sausage
- Some deli meats

As tasty as these items are, they are high in saturated fat — a cause of inflammation. You do not have to remove these from your or your teen's diet entirely. Instead, implement lifestyle practices that cut down on consumption.

Such practices include:

- Going meatless a few times a week.
- Consuming meat with only one meal per day.
- Treating meat as a side dish rather than the main course so that the quantity is reduced on your plate.

Items containing trans fats

Deep-fried foods, most processed foods, margarine . . . All of these contain trans fats. Foods that contain partially hydrogenated vegetable oil are the largest source of trans fats in modern diets. Such items are mass-produced because they have a long shelf life and are relatively cheap for manufacturers to produce.

Trans fat is naturally occurring and is produced in the gut of some animals and can be found in trace amounts in some animal products such as meat and milk products. However, for the most part, it is artificially made during the production of food. As a result, humanity is consuming trans fats in an unprecedented way that has not been seen throughout human history. It is leading to several negative effects, such as the increased risk of developing cardiovascular disease, diabetes, obesity, and inflammation.

Avoiding trans fats can be tricky since so many items contain them, but the surest way to do so is to read food labels carefully. Anything that has partially hydrogenated items on the ingredients list should be banned from your grocery cart. Trans fats are not always easy to spot on food labels. Some regular vegetable oils contain trans fats, but they may not be listed as such. Canola and soybean oils with a concentration of between 0.56% to 4.27% likely contain trans fat. If you're unsure about any item and its trans fat content, put it back and do some research. The best way to ensure you do not fall victim to the ill effects of trans fats is to reduce the amount of processed food in your household diet.

Foods That Help Calm Anxiety Symptoms

No food can cure anxiety, but implementing certain dietary changes can go a long way toward alleviating the symptoms. Before moving on to the specifics, we need to clarify something. Diet plays a big part in mental health. If you want to change your physical workouts or take supplements, you need to discuss this with your doctor beforehand to ensure it is safe to make these changes. The same goes for changing your teen's diet. It's also a good idea to involve a nutritionist to get some extra guidance. Your doctor can refer you to a reputable nutritionist in your area.

The effects of dietary change are often not immediately apparent. It is likely going to take your teen some time to adjust. Encourage your teenager to be patient and remind them that these changes are an overall improvement for good physical, mental, and emotional health. Anxiety symptoms are likely to slowly improve thanks to fewer ups and downs caused by the excess intake of sugar. Medications your teen takes also affect how soon relief from anxiety symptoms is gained. Again, this is something that your doctor can guide you on. Diet alone will not fix everything. An integrated treatment approach, including talk therapy, mindfulness techniques, stress relief, good sleep hygiene, exercise, and a balanced diet, are equally important parts of self-care.

Relating to the diet aspect of a holistic approach to self-care, consuming whole foods is the most practical approach. Whole foods are those that remain as close to the state found in nature. They do not have added preservatives, flavorings, colorings, sugars, or any other processed ingredients. They are the opposite of processed foods and are not normally found in factory environments. They are those that you would pick in your garden or find in the organic section of your local grocer. There is even a diet consisting of eating whole foods alone. The emphasis is on eating natural, healthy foods that improve overall health. Always remember that connection between the gastrointestinal tract and your brain. Put the good stuff into the stomach (and there's no doubt that whole foods are the best you can get), and the brain works better.

A whole-food diet provides you with the following:

- **Fiber**: This helps you feel fuller for longer and helps your body absorb sugars more slowly to stop fluctuations in energy and, thus, mood fluctuations. Fiber-rich foods include fruits, vegetables, whole grains, and legumes.

- **Antioxidants**: These are natural fighters of inflammation. Options include green leafy vegetables, turmeric (which will be discussed shortly), and berries. Even dark chocolate, which can be consumed occasionally, provides antioxidants.

- **Folate**: A type of B vitamin, aids in the production of dopamine. It can be sourced from lentils, leafy greens, and cantaloupe.

These are just a few of the elements you can extract from a whole foods diet that will help to alleviate anxiety symptoms.

Certain supplements also help reduce the symptoms of anxiety. The best practice is for your teen to get as much of their nutritional needs from whole food sources instead of pills and capsules. Still, it is better to ensure this nutritional value is included rather than risk going without it.

Magnesium is an essential nutrient for combating anxiety as it ensures serotonin is released adequately in the brain. Magnesium deficiencies can lead to anxiety attacks, and the stress of an attack only depletes the body further of this mineral. It is best to take magnesium before going to bed to help calm nerves and get better sleep quality. Foods that contain naturally occurring magnesium include legumes, nuts, seeds, and avocado.

Tryptophan is another supplement that promotes the production of serotonin. Tryptophan also encourages better sleep quality as well as eases the symptoms of mood swings. It is an essential amino acid present in foods like oats, nuts, seeds, cheese, milk, and canned tuna. The supplement is listed as L-tryptophan in your local pharmacy.

General Nutrition Recommendations for Managing Anxiety

Apart from the dos and don'ts stated above, here are a few dietary rules that help the anxiety sufferer:

Avoid stimulating substances like caffeine, alcohol, and nicotine

Teens often turn to cigarettes, alcohol, and coffee to escape anxiety symptoms. They seek to calm their nerves. They are looking for a safe space where these pressures are removed.

Stimulants do offer an escape in the immediate and short term. But withdrawal symptoms from any of the above-mentioned stimulants are reminiscent of anxiety. For example, nicotine in cigarettes raises blood pressure and heart rate, which simulates an anxiety attack. Alcohol may cause temporary slumber, but it disrupts good sleep cycles, initiating that vicious circle of sleep deprivation and anxious behavior. Caffeine gives that temporary boost of vivacity, but the subsequent jump in nerves is not worth the headache.

Drink enough water

Most sodas and fruit drinks have a high sugar content. These promote inflammation. The best drink for your anxious teen is water, or perhaps seltzer if they find water distasteful, provided it has no sugar. Not drinking enough water daily — at least 64 oz — leads to dehydration.

Signs of dehydration include:

- Headaches
- Weakness and muscle fatigue
- Lightheadedness
- Increased heart rate
- Restlessness
- Irritability

These are all symptoms that mimic anxiety. The stress of being deprived of adequate quantities of water to power brain cells leads to depression and anxiety. We must all drink enough water, the recommended value between 6 and 8 glasses daily. However, it is especially important for someone who is anxiety-prone to get that needed hydration. Drinking water can induce instant feelings of calm.

Get enough vitamin D

In this modern world, we spend most of our time indoors (at work, school, or home). This has led to a serious global vitamin D deficiency as we soak up the vitamin most often from the sun's rays. Even in Florida — one of the sunniest states in the USA — most people suffer from a vitamin D deficiency. Vitamin D is necessary for stabilizing mood — it improves your outlook and combats anxiety.

Make it a priority that your teen spends more time outdoors where they can soak up this essential vitamin. Vitamin D can also be supplemented with vitamin D3 capsules. Certain foods like salmon, eggs, and fortified milk also contain quantities of vitamin D. Mushrooms like maitake, reishi, and cordyceps are also good sources.

Eat foods rich in omega-3 fatty acids

There are three main types of fatty acids.

They are called:

- Alpha-linolenic acid (ALA)
- Eicosapentaenoic acid (EPA)
- Docosahexaenoic acid (DHA)

They all play a role in optimizing overall brain health. DHA is particularly relevant to maintaining the structural aspects of the brain, but it is EPA that most significantly helps reduce anxiety. It is an anti-inflammatory agent. Another function of omega-3s that helps to reduce anxiety includes normalizing the production of dopamine to stabilize mood.

Omega-3 fatty acids can be supplemented in your teen's diet through supplements containing high proportions of EPA, like cod liver oil and sustainable fish oil. Most people take fish oil in capsules because otherwise, the taste is less than ideal.

The most popular natural source of omega-3s is fatty fish like salmon, herring, mackerel, and sardines. The pink color of salmon is a result of the presence of an antioxidant known as astaxanthin. The antioxidant helps protect the omega-3 from oxidation and keeps their neuroprotective properties intact. Salmon and other fatty fish are particularly rich in EPA and DHA.

Plant sources of omega-3 include chia seeds and flax seeds. They contain ALA. ALA is a shorter-chain omega-3. It is converted into EPA and DHA at lower levels. EPA and DHA are more bioactive.

Include turmeric in your diet

This tip adds a little spice to your teen's life . . . pun intended. Turmeric has been celebrated for its medical benefits throughout history because of its active compound, curcumin. Curcumin is an antioxidant with anti-inflammatory properties. It also helps boost serotonin levels. Turmeric can be added to the diet through supplements or by adding this spice (which can also be found in curry powder) to dishes and smoothies. It can even be used to make tea.

Turmeric is safe to eat overall, but going overboard with the consumption can lead to feelings of nausea, vomiting, and upset stomach. I take curcumin in capsule form.

Eat more fermented foods

Foods preserved through the process of fermentation are probiotic-rich. Probiotics are good bacteria introduced to the gut intended to optimize the conditions in that environment. Particular strains such as Lactobacillus (L.) Plantarum is proven to balance intestinal microbe populations in human beings. This is found in several fermented foods like kefir, miso, sauerkraut, pickles, kimchi, tempeh, and brined olives.

Eat foods rich in zinc

Zinc is essential for maintaining the connection between the brain and the body. It is especially necessary for upkeeping the vagus nerve, which transports messages of calm to alleviate symptoms of anxiety. In addition, zinc is needed to produce feel-good hormones like serotonin and dopamine. Its presence also helps increase levels of brain-derived neurotrophic factor (BDNF) in areas of the brain that reign over emotions. Mood nosedives when BDNF is low so keeping it elevated is a must to defeat anxiety.

The human body cannot produce zinc. It must come through supplements or adding items like whole grains, oysters, kale, broccoli, legumes, and nuts to your teen's diet.

Eat three balanced meals a day and a healthy snack every few hours

We have established that high blood sugar induces anxiety. The opposite is also true. Low blood sugar is called hypoglycemia. It is caused most often by not eating enough and on time, conditions that place the body in a state of starvation. Signs of hypoglycemia include shakiness, heart palpitations, and sweating; signs that mirror anxiety and also cause it.

Your teen needs to find that healthy balance between not consuming too many simple carbohydrates and consuming too little. The easiest way to do this is to eat three balanced meals daily and eat nourishing and energizing snacks in between. It is commonplace for teens to do so but skipping breakfast sets your teen up for a day filled with anxiety-induced struggles. Starting the day off on the right foot with the nutrition the brain needs to function is best. It does not need to get complicated, either. Eating a fortified whole-grain cereal with low-fat milk and blueberries provide vitamin Bs, vitamin D, and protein to give that mental strength.

More examples of simple breakfast ideas to help your teen fight depression include:

- Smoothies created from banana, almond milk, and flaxseeds as a source of omega-3s.

- Full-fat Greek yogurt with honey and granola as a source of probiotics to prevent and reduce inflammation in the brain.

- Avocado toast (Avocado provides the right source of high fatty content to protect the brain.)

A few guidelines for achieving balance in your meals throughout the day include:

- Eat 7 to 8 servings of fruits and vegetables daily to get the vitamins and minerals needed to improve cognitive function, stabilize moods, and aid in memory and learning.

- Eat at least 3 to 4 ounces of protein with each meal. This is approximately one palm-size portion of protein. Options include poultry like chicken, dairy products like yogurt, fish, seafood, and lean meats like lamb. Vegetarians can opt for tofu or beans as a protein source.

- Eat complex carbohydrates and avoid simple carbohydrates.

Eat a healthy and balanced diet like the Mediterranean diet

As the name indicates, the Mediterranean diet is a way of eating that originated in the Mediterranean region.

The emphasis is on eating:

- Whole grains
- Fresh fruits and veggies
- Healthy fats like olive oil, avocados, and nuts
- Legumes
- Moderate amounts of seafood
- Low quantities of dairy and red meat

These foods are stacked in an organized system known as the Mediterranean Diet Pyramid. The first and most weighed tier highlights food you should consume daily and in every meal. This includes fruits, veggies, grains, beans, nuts, seeds, legumes, herbs, and spices. The next tier consists of fish and seafood, which should be eaten at least twice weekly. The final two tiers have poultry and dairy (consumption encouraged in moderate portions weekly) and meats and sweets, which should be eaten seldom. There is a decided avoidance of processed and refined foods. All these natural goodies provide the body with all the nutrition it needs. The Mediterranean diet is proven to prevent and lower the risk of developing several diseases and helps people live longer and healthier.

This way of eating has also been linked to lowered incidences and reduced symptoms of mental health conditions like depression and anxiety. This link is developed because the Mediterranean diet is anti-inflammatory. That property comes from the intake of plenty of fruits, veggies, and all the other components of the diet. The diet also helps combat anxiety by positively affecting sleep quality and cognitive performance.

I encourage you to do more research on the Mediterranean diet. In the meantime, to whet your appetite, here is a recipe for breakfast, lunch, and dinner. I didn't forget a healthy snack!

Herb, Tomato & Feta Egg Sandwich

The embodiment of what Mediterranean eating is about, this simple sandwich is packed with healthy ingredients like spinach and tomatoes.

Total Time: 20 Minutes | Cooking Time: 5 Minutes | Serving Size: 1 Sandwich | Makes: 4 Serving

INGREDIENTS

- 4 eggs, broken
- 4 multigrain sandwich thins
- 4 tsp extra virgin olive oil
- 1 tbsp fresh rosemary, snipped
- 2 cups fresh baby spinach
- 1 medium tomato, thinly sliced

- 4 tbsp reduced-fat feta cheese, crumbled
- Salt and black pepper to taste

DIRECTIONS

1. Preheat the oven to 375°F. Prepare a baking sheet by lining it with parchment paper.

2. Divide the sandwich thins and brush the insides with olive oil. Place on the prepared baking sheet and bake for 5 minutes or until the edges are lightly browned and crisp.

3. While the thins toast, heat 2 teaspoons of olive oil in a large skillet over medium heat. Add the rosemary and sauté until fragrant.

4. Add the eggs into the skillet one at a time. Cook for about 1 minute, so the whites are set, but the yolks still run.

5. Break the yolks with a spatula. Flip the eggs and cook for 1 more minute or until done. Remove the eggs from the heat.

6. Equally divide the spinach, then the tomato slices of the bottom halves of the toasted sandwich thins. Top each toasted bottom with an egg and one-quarter of the feta cheese. Sprinkle them with salt and pepper. Cover with the remaining sandwich thin.

7. Serve warm.

NUTRITIONAL INFORMATION PER SERVING

242 Calories; Protein 13 g; Carbohydrates 25 g; Dietary Fiber 6.2 g; Sugars 3.2 g; Fat 11.7 g; Saturated fat 2.9 g; Cholesterol 214 mg; Vitamin A 2448.4 IU; Vitamin C 12 mg; Folate 28.7 mcg; Calcium 123.2 mg; Iron 3 mg; Magnesium 9.9 mg; Potassium 143.8 mg; Sodium 501.2 mg

EXCHANGES

1 1/2 starch, 1 fat, 1 medium-fat protein, 1/2 vegetables

Mediterranean Chicken Wrap

Got leftover chicken tenders and couscous? Make tasty use of them with this easy-to-make yet refreshing lunch that gives a healthy dose of fresh herbs. The hint of lemony flavors never fails to brighten up a day. Elevate the healthy points this dish offers by serving it with a mixed green salad.

Total Time: 40 Minutes | Cooking Time: 15 Minutes | Serving Size: 1 Wrap | Makes: 4 Servings

INGREDIENTS

- 1 lb chicken tenders
- 4 10-inch wraps or tortillas (I prefer the spinach or sun-dried tomato variety)
- ⅓ cup whole-wheat couscous
- 3 tbsp extra-virgin olive oil
- 1 cup fresh parsley, chopped

- ½ cup fresh mint, chopped
- ¼ cup lemon juice
- ½ cup water
- 1 medium tomato, chopped
- 1 cup cucumber, chopped
- 2 tsp minced garlic
- ¼ tsp salt, divided
- ¼ tsp freshly ground black pepper

DIRECTIONS

1. Prepare the couscous by bringing the water to a boil in a small pot. Stir in the couscous and immediately remove the pot from the heat. Cover and allow to stand for 5 minutes before fluffing with a fork. Set the couscous aside while you move on to the next step.

2. In a small bowl, combine parsley, mint, lemon juice, oil, garlic, and half of the salt and pepper.

3. Toss chicken tenders, 1 tablespoon of the parsley mixture, and the remaining salt in a bowl.

4. Heat the tenders in a nonstick skillet and cook over medium heat for about 4 minutes per side or until cooked through. Allow to cool enough to handle.

5. Transfer the cooked chicken to a cutting board and slice it into bite-size pieces.

6. Combine the remaining parsley mixture, couscous, tomato, and cucumber.

7. Assemble the wraps by equally dividing the couscous mixture and spreading it onto each wrap. Do the same with the chicken. Roll the wraps up like a burrito. Tuck the sides in to keep the ingredients within.

8. Cut in half to serve. Can be refrigerated for later.

Keeping the filling inside a wrap or burrito is almost impossible, especially when hustling and bustling about. Solve that problem by wrapping the rollup in foil before you cut it in half. You can peel back the foil when you're eating for a no-mess lunch.

NUTRITIONAL INFORMATION PER SERVING

510 Calories; Protein 32.3 g; Carbohydrates 54.9 g; Dietary Fiber 5.7 g; Sugars 4.5 g; Fat 17.9 g; Saturated fat 3.3 g; Cholesterol 62.7 mg; Vitamin A 2026.5 IU; Vitamin C 32.8 mg; Folate 192 mcg; Calcium 165 mg; Iron 6.1 mg; Magnesium 59.1 mg; Potassium 564.2 mg; Sodium 725.6 mg; Thiamine 0.4 mg

EXCHANGES

3 starch, 4 lean meat, 2 fat

Pesto Chicken Salad with Green Salad

Total Time: 30 Minutes | Cooking Time: 15 Minutes | Serving Size: 2 Cups Greens plus ½ Cup Pesto Chicken Salad | Makes: 4 Servings

INGREDIENTS

- 1 lb boneless, skinless chicken breast, trimmed
- ¼ cup pesto
- ¼ cup low-fat mayonnaise
- 3 tbsp red onion, finely chopped
- 2 tbsp extra-virgin olive oil
- 2 tbsp red wine vinegar
- 1 5-ounce package (approximately 8 cups) mixed salad greens
- 1 pint grape or cherry tomatoes, halved
- Salt and pepper to taste

DIRECTIONS

1. Add the chicken and enough water to cover it by 1 inch to a saucepan. Bring the water to a boil over medium heat. Cover the saucepan and reduce the heat to low. Simmer for 10 to 15 minutes or until the chicken is no longer pink in the middle. Transfer the chicken to a clean cutting board. Allow the chicken to cool enough to handle. Shred into bite-size pieces.
2. Combine the pesto, mayonnaise, and red onion in a bowl.
3. Add the chicken. Toss. Ensure it is thoroughly coated.

4. Create a vinaigrette by whisking oil, vinegar, salt, and pepper together in a large bowl. Add the greens and tomatoes. Toss to coat.

5. To serve, share the green salad among 4 plates and equally top it with the chicken salad.

NUTRITIONAL INFORMATION PER SERVING

Carbohydrates 9.2 g; Dietary Fiber 2.3 g; Sugars 3.2 g; Fat 19.7 g; Saturated Fat 4.1 g; Cholesterol 71.4 mg; Vitamin A 1777.3 IU; Vitamin C 17.6 mg; Folate 57.4 mcg; Calcium 153 mg; Iron 2.1 mg; Magnesium 47.5 mg; Potassium 542.2 mg; Sodium 453.9 mg; Thiamine 0.1 mg; Added Sugar 1 g

EXCHANGES

1 vegetable, 3 1/2 lean meat, 3 fat

Crusted Fish Sticks

Total Time: 15 Minutes | Cooking Time: 15 Minutes | Serving Size: 1 | Makes: 1 Serving

INGREDIENTS

- 4 cod filets (can be fresh or defrosted)
- 4 tsp Dijon mustard
- 2 cups pretzels

DIRECTIONS

1. Preheat the oven to 400°F. Prepare a baking sheet by lining it with foil. Place a cooling rack on top to create a baking rack.

2. Remove thin bits at the ends of the filets and cut them into even sticks.

3. Crush the pretzels by placing them in a plastic bag and gently rolling them with a rolling pin. You also have the option of doing this in a food processor, but the process leaves more of a mess. Save yourself the cleanup and go with the first option. Pour the crumbs into a small bowl, a plate, or onto wax paper on the countertop.

4. Coat each filet with Dijon mustard, then press firmly into the pretzel crumbs to create a thick crust.

5. Place the filet pieces onto the backing rack. Bake for 15 to 18 minutes or until the fish stick is cooked through and flaky.

6. Serve warm with baked fries and your favorite dipping sauces.

NUTRITIONAL INFORMATION PER SERVING

For each cod fillet

Calories 212; Total Fat 1.79 g; Sat Fat 0.15 g; Trans Fat 0; Cholesterol 49 mg; Sodium 588 mg; Potassium 44 mg Total Carbohydrate 23.93 g Dietary Fiber 0.9 g Sugar 0.83 g Protein 23.1 g

Now that we have established how good lifestyle practices such as healthy eating can be used to combat anxiety, we are going to move on to therapies that can be used to compound the good effects experienced. But first, I want you to read an interview I did with a teenager who has anxiety. She uses the very therapeutic techniques we are going to discover together to manage her anxiety.

CHAPTER 4

She Speaks: A Teen's Anxiety Story

There is no better evidence of the hardships an anxious teen goes through or how effective coping techniques and behavioral therapies are than getting the testimonial straight from the source's mouth. I present to you Emma P. She is a lovely young lady to whom I had the honor of speaking. She answers the question that is so difficult to ask—*What is it like being a teen with anxiety?*

I hope that her answers give you insight into the mind of your anxious teen as well as the potential effectiveness of treatments. Here are her words—raw and unfiltered . . .

LM: Tell me about yourself.

EP: I'm going into 8th grade. I ran track for most of my life. I recently stopped due to a knee injury but also because my mental health took a turn. Now I do lacrosse as a goalie. I have a brother and sister, and I live with my mom and dad. I also have a dog.

LM: What are your hobbies?

EP: I love to read, hike with my dog, and bake.

LM: Do they help with your anxiety?

EP: Yes, reading does.

LM: What is school like for you? Is it a source of anxiety?

EP: Yes, it is a source of anxiety, both socially and academically. There is a lot of social pressure from peers. Pressure to succeed in school and also to do crazy things like ditching, pranks, food fights, etc.

LM: How about social media? Do you use that frequently?

EP: I use Snapchat.

LM: Do you think that causes anxiety?

EP: Yes. Right now, I am not at home, and my friends are all hanging out without me. I know this because they posted on social media. And I thought, "Oh my goodness, I'm not going to be their friend next year because I'm never there." I spend the summer in a different state than them each year. I'm in a group chat with them, and they call me, which does alleviate some of the anxiety of losing them.

LM: If you don't mind me asking, what is your official diagnosis/diagnoses?

EP: I struggle with depression and anxiety. I have had anxiety my whole life. My anxiety is overthinking and spiraling deep inside my head. I struggle a lot with stress. My therapist thinks I may have ADHD related to my anxiety as well. I'm starting to do better in terms of depression. I am "starting to see the light again." I was on medication, and it wasn't working. That definitely caused a lot of anxiety in my body. I thought, "Oh no, this isn't working.

What am I going to do?" I had to remind myself that this medication isn't for everyone, and I simply had to find something that works.

LM: Do you have anyone else in your family, life, relatives, or friends that suffers from anxiety?

EP: To be honest, I think we all do. Everyone in the world. But in my family, yes, my dad definitely, as well as my sister, brother, and mother. I've noticed things that trigger them. I think my mom, as a mother, worries a lot. There is a thin line between worrying and anxiety, in my opinion. My sister is going to be a junior in high school. She struggles with academic anxiety. She is going to a great school, but it is very stressful. She is also going through a medical condition called endometriosis. It has impacted her life and the rest of the family greatly. We all feel helpless when she is screaming in pain at 2 am. I needed to feel in control over something, and I just couldn't.

LM: I think that a big part of anxiety is a feeling of a lack of control.

EP: Yeah. Lately, I felt I couldn't get control of anything. Especially when COVID hit. I had no control of my life. Fifth grade was the start of my depression. I lost everything. I missed the last year of elementary school and graduation. It meant a lot to me. I was the lead role in our play, and I had worked so hard for it. Then COVID hit, and the show was canceled. I was a runner and had made it to the Junior Olympics. I was so excited. Then that was canceled. That one hit home. I had worked so hard and got nothing in return. I stayed in my room all day, wasn't eating as much, exercising as much. I just went down. People on social media say, "If you have depression, just become happy." I kept thinking that something was wrong with me. I couldn't make myself happy. That definitely sparked anxiety in me. I couldn't be there for my family in a time that was brutal for everyone. Then I felt guilty. Because people were out there dying every day, and I am just sitting in my room unhappy, and the situation was not comparable.

LM: You're an empath.

EP: Yes, I am. So that's when I got my therapist, Dr. S. We have worked together for a bit over a year and a half now.

LM: Was that your first time in therapy?

EP: Oh no, I have been in therapy since second grade.

LM: Specifically for anxiety?

EP: Second grade was a rough grade for me. I wasn't making friends, and I had anger and issues controlling my emotions. In second grade, I talked to guidance counselors at school. I went to two therapists between second and third grade but didn't stick with any of them. I have gone through my fair share of therapists, social workers, and guidance counselors. That fact does trigger anxiety for me. There are all these stories of people saying I went to this therapy for the first time, and I fell in love with the therapist. They fit so right for me. I am still finding that person for me, and it makes me question what is wrong with me. That is a major question I have struggled with my whole life. "What is wrong with me?" My current therapist has helped me so much when I was spiraling into depression. She gave me tools and guidance. She helped me out of the darkness. It definitely helped me to talk with someone. I don't think of my therapists as doctors or adults with degrees, I think of them as friends to whom I can vent and cry.

LM: That's good for other teens to hear. An important lesson is that there is nothing wrong with you; your increased anxiety is wrong, not you. I also think it is important for teenagers and parents to hear that when starting therapy, the first few therapists you try may not be the right fit. That does not mean there is anything wrong with YOU. Finding the right one takes time.

EP: I am still realizing that to this day. I talk often with a family friend. He says that anxiety will never go away or disappear, and that is not a bad thing. There is such a thing as a good amount of anxiety and too much anxiety. A lot of people struggle with way too much anxiety, and they are drowning. You need anxiety to live. If you don't have anxiety, you are dead in a minute. You might think it's fun to go jump off a roof if anxiety is not present to stop you.

LM: Or go pet that fluffy black bear you see in the woods.

EP: Exactly. For a while, I was in denial. I thought I had a normal amount of anxiety. But that anxiety stopped me from going outside and hanging out with friends because I felt betrayed from my elementary school years. My anxiety caused me to think I wasn't good enough. That no one would ever like me. Seventh grade was really good for me but also tough. I did have to battle anxiety with my whole mental capacity. I was exhausted every day. Not from exercise but from shutting the door on my brain to stop all the anxiety from piling in. At that point, anxiety overruled my brain. I had no other thought process. It was just anxiety. If we went out for ice cream as a family, which even then was a huge step for me, I questioned every decision I made. Whether it was what ice creams to choose or where to sit. All the options gave me a lot of anxiety. What if I choose the wrong flavor or the wobbly table?

LM: You were afraid to make a mistake.

EP: Yeah, I was terrified of making a mistake and someone using it against me.

LM: What age were you when you first started to experience anxiety? Do you remember where you were or what you were doing? What were your first symptoms, and how did they evolve over time?

EP: I believe my first symptoms were a loss of connection.

LM: What do you mean by that?

EP: My anxiety, to this day, causes a loss of connection. I consider it a symptom. I lose friendships.

LM: Are you describing isolation?

EP: Yeah, that is a way better word for it. It started when I was in 2nd grade, so I was about 6 or 7. My anxiety was always there, but it truly sparked to life when I tried making a friend. As the emotional person that I am, I came up to this classmate and said, "Hey, do you want to be friends?" She said, "No." That basically stopped my friendship search. I put myself out on the line and got rejected. I don't know why. I still question myself today.

These two questions run through my head: "What did I do wrong?" and "What is wrong with me?" Those two questions have stayed with me my whole life. They have evolved over time into "What's wrong with my body image?" "What's wrong with the way I talk?" "The way I identify?" "My school grades?" "Am I being judged for my family's actions?" It continues to evolve into so much more. Those questions spiral around in my head. As a 13-year-old, I think I know the world, but I don't. I wish I did, but I don't. Because of those questions, I lost control of my whole life. I needed control over something or someone. I chose someone. I became mean. I kept everyone out. My family, especially my mother. I kept her inside a tiny loop. If someone said something unkind, I didn't sit back. I stood up for myself. Sometimes that's good, but it set me back in the friendship game. I just lost it. Every day. I went about my day, and if I heard something about me, you knew where I was going to be. I was going to be right up in their face, and I was going to be honest with them. This didn't help my anxiety in any way, shape, or form. If anything, it created more questions. "Emma, what is wrong with you?" "What are you doing?" "You're going crazy!"

LM: Looking back, do you have any regrets? Maybe something anxiety caused you to do? A therapy you wished you had tried sooner?

EP: I definitely have regrets.

LM: I want you to know I am not placing blame.

EP: I know. I regret putting a wall up. I put a 7 ft steel wall around me. I was untouchable. If someone even touched my wall, I would attack, and I regret doing that. I regret not understanding that everyone is going through their own things. Everyone is trying to survive. People don't think this, but elementary school is really tough. You are with these kids for the rest of your life unless you move. I regret showing up every day and blocking people out.

LM: I'm sure you were trying to protect yourself and preserve your sanity, which was needed at the time.

EP: What I regret about this is I never took down the wall.

LM: So, you would say it's still up?

EP: It's probably a 4 ft steel wall now.

LM: That's progress.

EP: It is progress. I do shave a layer off periodically. I have been bullied, and my 7 ft steel wall definitely helped keep my guard and a straight face on. But the people who tried to be friends, I regret that solely. Because I probably impacted their lives a lot, like that girl did to me when I asked her to be my friend. That was a decision I made out of anxiety. I was thinking about myself and not others. You should think about others and how you could impact them. I solely regret hurting others, being selfish, and being stuck in my head.

LM: Do you know what specific therapy you have had for anxiety? CBT, DBT, ACT?

EP: My therapist used CBT techniques with me.

LM: Could you name some lessons you have learned from your experience with anxiety?

EP: I think a lesson I have learned is I am not crazy; I am just me. I am a person who has emotions and feelings. I am not a crazy or terrible person. I might be a little more aggressive, but that is who I am, and no one can change that. I shouldn't have to change that, either.

LM: That's a big revelation. The fact that you are not anxiety, you are a person with anxiety. It is a part of you, but it does not define you.

EP: Somedays, I feel like I am nothing but depression or anxiety, but then I think back to my therapy sessions, and I rephrase it. If I am afraid of these things, I am a victim being fed on. It took me a while to stand up for myself mentally and say, "Nothing is wrong with you." I think that was the hardest sentence to ever say. Now I can confidently say it. I have learned that my anxiety and depression are a part of me and do not define me. I am learning to be proud of them. They have shaped me into who I am today.

LM: It sounds like you would probably say on a scale from 1–10 that your anxiety has been at a 10 in the past (**EP:** Yes), but where would you say it is now? I recognize it fluctuates day-to-day, but what would you say the average is?

EP: I would say a 5. So, 50%.

LM: Would you say you have made progress?

EP: I would say I have made a ton of progress.

LM: What would you say has been the biggest aid in making that progress?

EP: My dog. I often come home to him after school and cry on him. He sits on my bed, and it brings me joy to know he is there. For a more definitive answer, what has helped me the most is sleep. I go to bed early, falling asleep easily, but I wake up all night long. I started taking melatonin, and I woke up and had a better day.

LM: Sleep is so important. It's one of the fundamentals of treatment, along with nutrition and exercise.

EP: Some people skip past it and say, "I'll run on caffeine," but sleep has helped me so much mentally. I used to be scared to sleep because it left me alone with my thoughts.

LM: Many can relate to that.

EP: Each day, I would exhaust myself to the brink, so I would fall asleep superfast. I got on this cycle of going and going, and then I broke. Then I slept the entire night. I woke up the next day, and I was like, "Wow. I have the energy to get out of bed and shower and make myself breakfast."

LM: I know you exercise regularly; would you say that helps too?

EP: Yes, that definitely helps. I have gone through stages where I don't exercise, and it has taken a toll on my mental health.

LM: Have you tried things like meditation, relaxation or breathing exercises, coping skills, etc.?

EP: Yes. I work with a yoga teacher one-on-one weekly. She is like another therapist of mine. She takes me through a relaxation progression called Yoga Nidra, which is like a body scan that puts my body to sleep within 20 minutes, and I do not wake up all night long. I also do meditation.

LM: How do you do it? Through an app or online?

EP: Sometimes, I do it in my head. I do square breathing. Breathe in for 4, hold for 4, breathe out for 4, etc. I also take 3 deep breaths every day, and this helps me stay centered and calm. If I want to do more, there is an app called Headspace. It has meditations I have used multiple times. YouTube is also my go-to thing. I have fallen asleep watching Bob Ross paint. This is something I do regularly. YouTube also has body scans and Yoga Nidra. It's not in person, but I can look up what I am wanting that night, and it is so helpful.

LM: That's great advice for teens.

EP: I don't wait for an adult to fix me; I do my part in the whole situation.

LM: What would you say to other teens about your experience with anxiety and what happens after you begin to get better from anxiety?

EP: Anxiety is not a one-and-done thing.

LM: I agree.

EP: What I would say to other teens is that anxiety is always there, but it is how you handle it that matters. On the road to recovering from severe anxiety, it's always going to be there, and you have to work hard to keep it at bay. It is a mental strain at first. I had to take mental health days at first because I was so mentally exhausted, and that is completely ok. It is ok if you are struggling, but you yourself need to find help or help yourself. You can't give up. With anxiety, I have found that it gets better, but I still have my bad days. You have to fight for yourself. It will get better. It is a process, and it does take time, but looking back, I am so glad that I took the mental health days. The hard days when I wanted to give up, I'm glad I didn't because I'm in a much better place. You have to work with yourself, and that scared me so much. To actually go into my brain and think. It was the biggest obstacle I had to overcome. I would tell other teenagers to put themselves first and go through their brains, whether with a therapist or alone. It helped me to go back through my traumas and describe them and realize I did do things wrong, but I don't need to hold on to those things. You don't have to hold on to things unless you want to. There is a difference between a want and a need.

LM: How are your relationships with your family and friends now?

EP: Friendship-wise, they are 30 times better. I found a group of friends that also struggle with anxiety and depression. I am always here for them to talk to and vice versa. I found a group of friends who show up when things aren't easy. It is amazing. I also have the most supportive parents ever. I am so grateful that they let me take mental health days, help me find therapists, and get food that nourishes my body that I also enjoy. Right now, I have so much help that I haven't even realized from my family. My family and friendships have been the best they have ever been.

LM: I think you said you were 6 years old when you started to experience anxiety. Did your family notice right away?

Did they realize it was anxiety, and how did they react? Did their actions help or create more challenges for you?

EP: They figured it out because I overreacted in school, and they started to question my mental health. Because my sister didn't go through anxiety as severely as I did, I don't think my parents truly knew what was happening, but they learned. When they got that call that I was acting out at school, we had a talk. I cried; my mom cried. Ever since then, they have been supportive and did research into symptoms and treatments. It probably triggers anxiety for them as well, but they keep telling me that they can handle their own stuff. Whether they are waking me up in the morning, they are always there helping me. In the beginning, it was awkward because none of our family members had gone through this before. But they found a way to manage it with therapy sessions and talking to me as a mom and dad and a friend.

LM: It obviously sounds like you have had a huge amount of support and have been lucky enough to have been in therapy. One of the reasons I am writing this book is for people who don't have access to mental health care, either due to finances or accessibility. Thank you for your time and your wonderful insights.

EP: You're welcome.

We highly value your thoughts and feedback!

Support and reviews help my book reach more families with anxious teens. You can leave a review on Amazon by scanning the QR code or using the link in your order if you live in a non-listed country.

Please follow these simple steps to rate/review my book:
1. Open your phone camera.
2. Hover it over the QR code above.
3. Leave a review for my book.

All it takes is 60 seconds to make a difference!

CHAPTER 5
CBT I: Fact or Feeling?

Lifestyle changes are a great and necessary start to stopping the torment inflicted by anxiety. Those changes are not the end of the road, though. They are simply the foundation. Often, the benefits of such adjustments will not be realized until treatment is also implemented. Anxiety among teens is prevalent and impairing. Treatment is not an option if your teenager has been struggling with anxiety for 6 months or longer. It is a must. This treatment needs to align with the developmental concerns of adolescents. Cognitive-behavioral therapy (CBT) is the primary psychological treatment for anxiety disorders in youths.

What Is Cognitive Behavioral Therapy?

Despite the long-winded nature of the word, you can think of CBT as goal-oriented talk therapy. The formal term for talk therapy is psychotherapy. This vocal expression aims to make the connection between thoughts, feelings, and behaviors apparent.

Your teen is a newcomer to this physical plane of life. Most teens are still trying to understand themselves. They are still trying to get to the core of what makes them . . . well, them. In trying to figure things out, thoughts and feelings get jumbled up inside them. It is hard to tell one thought or feeling from the other. It is hard to identify the source of these things within. Often, the difficulty compounds itself, especially when anxiety enters the picture. Negative thinking swirls into the mix, bringing with it uncertainty and fear. Anxiety turns every thought into a catastrophe, and it does not leave room to examine the legitimacy or accuracy of those thoughts.

But talking things out allows for separating these tangled threads. Talking things out serves as a map for your teen to discover thoughts and feelings they didn't know existed within them. This discovery lets them have more control. It lets them see why they act in some of the ways they do, and so, control of self (thoughts, feelings, and behavior) is more attainable. CBT brings awareness, and that is the most powerful tool one can have to overcome anxiety. Awareness lets your teen challenge these negative thoughts to see more clearly through their dark veil.

The roots of CBT as a treatment for mental illnesses started sprouting in the early 1900s when pioneers like psychologist B.F. Skinner (1904 – 1990), the Nobel-prize-winning psychologist, physiologist, and experimental neurologist, Ivan Pavlov (1849 – 1936), and psychologist, John B. Watson (1878 – 1958) developed several theories relating to behavioral approaches to such treatments. Their theories were based on the idea that behaviors were measurable, modeled, and, thus, changeable. Their ideas paved the way for the first implementations of such therapies to help WWII veterans who suffered from psychological issues upon returning from the war.

Aaron T. Beck developed the first true model of CBT in 1964. He was an American psychologist who treated people with psychological issues like depression. After years of research, he noticed certain patterns in his patients. They tended to have negative views of themselves, the people around them, and their outlook on the future. No matter how much time he spent exploring their past with them, this negative view persisted. He theorized that perhaps holding on to this negative view might be the reason why a person was depressed, and so, the simplest form of CBT was born.

Beck understood there was a link between thoughts and feelings. They influenced how a person perceived events and, thus, how they behaved in response. This happened even if they were unaware of those thoughts and feelings. Even to this day, this idea is valid. It is not the situation at hand that determines how a person feels about it. Rather, it is how this person interprets that situation that determines how they feel. The same set of circumstances might occur to many individuals, but they will all feel and act differently because they all interpret what's going on differently. Beck noted that his depressed patients consistently had negative interpretations of events because of their tendency toward negative thinking.

Cognitive behavioral therapy has evolved over the decades, but one focus remains the same—reshaping the way people with psychological issues think to a more positive outlook. It is not just used to treat depression but also relationship problems, substance use disorders, and, of course, anxiety. With this reshaped view, the sufferer of such a problem gains self-awareness so that improved emotional and mental functioning is achieved. It gives this person the tools to function healthily here and now despite facing troubling circumstances. This reframing relies on what is called the ABC model.

The ABC Model and How It Works

The ABC model was developed by researcher and psychologist Albert Ellis (1913 – 2007). He developed a therapy called Rational-Emotive Behavior Therapy (REBT) in the 1950s. The rationale behind this therapy was the identification of the unreasonable and ungrounded negative thoughts and beliefs that led to the development of behavioral and emotional issues. REBT is the precursor to CBT. Even today, REBT is noted as a subset of CBT as the ABC model is a core component of CBT.

The letters of the ABC stand for the following:

- **A – Activating agent**

    This may also be referred to as the antecedent or adversity. It is the event that triggers the process. It can be a major event like witnessing or being part of a traumatic incident. But, more often, it is simpler and more subtle, like a person speaking rudely to you or a raised voice not even addressing you.

- **B – Beliefs**

    This determines the outcome of the adversity. There are two types of beliefs:

    1. **Irrational beliefs**. These are not logical and are extreme. For example, an irrational belief may be that someone raising their voice to you means that person hates you or that you are an unlovable person. Such beliefs are rigid, with no room for any other way of thinking.

    2. **Rational beliefs**. They are not extreme and are logical. They are also flexible, allowing for consideration of other points of view. A rational belief about someone yelling at you might be that this person is having a bad day and their actions have nothing to do with your self-worth. Rational beliefs allow a person not to internalize events outside of themselves.

    Rational beliefs allow for healthy emotions that are adaptive. A person with such a belief system does not awfulize events, is self-accepting, and accepts others. Still, their emotions are not always positive, and that is okay. Sometimes, negative emotions like concern, sadness, and annoyance are necessary for the healthy processing of some events. Always remember that the ABC model (and CBT, for that matter) is not based on getting rid of negative emotions. It is about gaining awareness of them to process them in a healthy, sensible way.

- **C – Consequence**

This is a person's feelings or actions in response to the activating event. The consequences are determined by one's beliefs.

A more visual view of the model looks like this:

Activating event (trigger) → Belief → Consequence (emotions, reactions)

In this model, B links A and C, so, challenging negative and irrational beliefs is the focus of CBT. By changing irrational beliefs, which fuel disorders like anxiety, more positive consequences can be created.

Often, negative thoughts, based on irrational thinking, are an automatic response. This natural inclination to think in such a way only worsens the emotional difficulties experienced, having a destructive influence on one's mood and outlook. The most tragic part is the lack of awareness that this is happening. CBT helps people like your teen learn to identify not only that this is occurring but also their particular negative thought patterns. Once identification is made, you can challenge and then replace those thoughts with more realistic and objective thoughts that improve your outlook and quality of life.

Identification is not a one-off incident. It sets the precedent for self-monitoring so that the most common (automatic) thoughts are known. To be clear, common thoughts are not evils that must be completely banished. Our brain is *supposed* to make jumps and assumptions. These help us stay safe and healthy. Only a small percentage of cognitive distortions impair mood.

Cognitive distortions take on many forms, like:

- Filtering – Focusing solely on the negative while ignoring the positives.
- Catastrophizing – Constantly expecting the worst-case scenario to occur.
- Needing to always be right – Being right overrides everything else, and even the idea of being wrong is repugnant.
- Jumping to conclusions – Arriving at conclusions based on little or no evidence.
- Blaming – Does not accept personal responsibility and assumes that everyone else is liable.
- Emotional reasoning – Believes that emotions are the basis for reality and truth.
- Personalizing – Acting with the assumption of self-responsibility at all times.
- Polarized thinking – Taking on an all-or-nothing mindset with no tolerance for gray areas. Such a mindset ignores complexities (also known as Black-and-White Thinking).
- Control fallacies – Assuming that either only others are to blame or only oneself is to be blamed if problems arise.

- The fallacy of fairness – Acting with the assumption that life should always be fair

- Overgeneralizing – Using the outcome of one situation as a rule for all other situations.

- Heaven's Reward Fallacy – Acting with the expectation that sacrificing oneself will be rewarded.

- The fallacy of change – Banking on change from other people.

- "Shoulds" – Holding on to an extreme code of conduct and judging others and oneself if any of these rules are broken.

- Global labeling – Reaching conclusions about many instances based on one instance.

Negative thoughts are specific to the situation at hand and can be changed as your teen learns to rewire their brain. It is core beliefs that are deeply ingrained and offer more resistance to change because they tend to form early in life or through traumatic events. They are the items that take on absolute status in the mind when we think. Noting negative thoughts helps detect irrational beliefs. Even though harder to reframe, these beliefs can be molded into more realistic and positive conclusions.

CBT vs. Psychodynamic Therapy

Before we move into more specifics about cognitive behavioral therapy, let's address an elephant that you might find in the room when you do more research about this topic. Sometimes, CBT is confused with psychodynamic therapy.

Psychodynamic therapy is an exploration of the mind to facilitate a deeper understanding of a person's emotions and their associated mental processes. Like CBT, it is a form of talk therapy. It is primarily used to treat depression and a few other serious psychological disorders where people find out they have lost meaning throughout their daily life. Also called psychodynamic counseling, the approach seeks to help people find patterns in their thoughts, beliefs, and emotions so they can gain better insight into where this lack of purpose stems from. Awareness helps them find their way back to living life with direction.

Our present thoughts and emotions are influenced by the past, whether we know it or not. Our behaviors arise due to both conscious and unconscious motives. As such, psychodynamic therapy stresses the exploration of childhood experiences and how they influence our thoughts, emotions, and behaviors as adults. For the sufferer of the psychological disorder to gain the most benefit from this explanation, a deep bond founded on trust must be developed between this person and the therapist. Even this relationship needs to be examined during the process to show how it reflects, contrasts, and is similar to other relationships that this person has.

Psychodynamic therapy was very popular but has been largely pushed to the side since CBT gained popularity over the last few years. However, the effectiveness of this type of talk therapy cannot be denied, and it is still a very popular and favored type of talk therapy. The main difference between the two therapies is the focus. CBT is present-focused, with a spotlight placed on behavior and thought patterns that are not beneficial to your teen. On the other hand, psychodynamic therapy focuses on the past and relationships to determine why emotional and mental issues arise in the present.

Psychodynamic Therapy vs. CBT

The table below summarizes the differences between the two forms of talk therapy.

Psychodynamic Therapy	CBT
Requires a deep delve into the past and thus is a long-term approach with open-ended therapy.	Has a specific goal in mind and is brief and time-limited.
Focuses on the past to solve issues arising in the present.	Is primarily focused on the present.
Highlights how the past creates current issues.	Highlights how thoughts create a cycle that produces your current issues.
Sessions are led by the client and are less structured.	Sessions are led by the therapist and are structured.
Is session-based.	Is session-based. The client has homework and practices specific skills between sessions.
Is focused on the client-therapist relationship.	Focuses on the individual.

The two types of talk therapy are not mutually exclusive. CBT is a type of psychotherapy. It is used to make connections between feelings, thoughts, and behaviors. As a result, psychotherapists often use CBT to help first identify and then correct dysfunctional patterns in thoughts and feelings, and so, how a person acts out.

Psychodynamic therapy requires the use of a licensed therapist as there is such a heavy focus on the relationship between that person and the client. CBT is also best performed by a licensed therapist who specializes in that type of therapy. However, some aspects of the talk therapy can be done at home. There is even some evidence to support the effectiveness of self-directed computer-based CBT apps and AI.

Features of CBT

CBT umbrellas several talk therapies and shares characteristics with others. As such, it might be difficult to identify. However, understanding its components eliminates these uncertainties.

Those features are:

Emotional responsive

A notable pillar in developing the CBT approach is the concept that thoughts are influenced by feelings. Changing how a patient feels means addressing the way they interpret (think about) and so, react to triggering situations. Having the ability to objectively look at how we analyze situations, as well as developing control of how we respond, goes a long way in helping us feel better.

Employs understanding and rationale

Thinking and feeling go hand-in-hand. As such, to improve mood, CBT relies on encouraging patients to reason their way through situations that would have previously triggered negative thinking. It helps to remove emotions from the driver's seat of the mind's vehicle and instead places cognition in control.

Time-limited

Sessions between a patient and a therapist trained to guide patients through CBT typically range between 5 and 20 sessions. This is a sharp contrast to other talk therapies like psychodynamic therapy, which is open-ended with no definitive end date. Several factors influence the exact number of sessions scheduled.

Some include:

- The nature of the targeted problem.
- The patient.
- The patient's goal.
- The resources available to the patient.

Because of the brief nature of CBT, patients often use the guidance of a therapist for a short time and then apply the CBT strategies learned on their own with additional support. If the problem persists or another arises, then it may be best to apply a different type of therapy to target specific traumas and barriers to healthy mental and emotional function.

Collaborative

At its best, CBT is performed with a patient developing a relationship with a licensed, experienced therapist well-versed in the practice. This relationship will only yield fruitful results if the patient believes the therapist has their best interest at heart while leading them down this path. That is only to be expected with the personal nature of talking your way through the intricacies of your thoughts.

As such, if you seek out the guidance of a therapist to lead your teen through this talk therapy, ensure this is someone your anxious teen trusts, respects, and feels comfortable with. Otherwise, you will likely be throwing money down the drain as your teen will not confide in this person the way they should to get out of the trap of negative thinking. It is important to note, as you saw in Emma P's story, the first therapist you visit may not be the right fit for your teenager. That is common and not a reason to give up. Persevere and find another therapist that is a better match. Trust me, I know how hard it is to start fresh with a new therapist, but once you find the right person for the job, you and your child will be so glad you did.

Structured with active engagement

A patient must develop a specific goal for using CBT. The therapist may help highlight this goal. The professional will then use specific tools and methodologies in each session to reach that goal by the end of the period scheduled with the patient. CBT sessions are tailored to the specific needs of each patient.

The Benefits of CBT

With these components leading to how CBT is approached, the practice offers a few unique benefits. The first and foremost is allowing the patient to develop healthier thinking patterns. This happens by first creating awareness of irrational beliefs. Irrational beliefs do not benefit your anxious teen in any way, shape, or form. It does not coincide with reality and instills harsh thoughts like, "I must get 100% on this test, or I am no good to anyone," or "I am ugly because I do not weigh the same as this influencer" because of reasons that have no foundation or basis in reality. But anxiety feeds on such thoughts, making it hard to see past the mistruths and creating a cycle where negative thinking also feeds on anxiety. This veil keeps your teen from being happy and healthy.

Negative thinking is insidious. It does not want to be discovered as lies and so detecting these patterns is not easy. However, it is possible. It starts with detecting these rigid boundaries that the patterns have set. Often, negative thinking comes in the form of internal statements that include words like 'must' and 'should.'

Irrational thoughts make you feel down on yourself, others, and life in general. Teach your teen to notice these feelings and hence trace the thoughts that generated them, whether or not the thoughts take an easily identifiable structure. Once such a thought is isolated, challenge it. Ask . . . does this belief make sense? Is it consistent with reality and facts that can be proven with concrete evidence? If that belief does coincide with reality, does this belief help or hinder me in achieving my goals in the long run? If reality supports it, is there another belief that aids me more than this belief? Can it be replaced with the more beneficial one?

Debate these thoughts and put up a fight when they try to bring you down. They lose their steam when you challenge them. As their strength diminishes, you are freed of their brutal consequences.

Questioning yourself paves the way to a new way of thinking. This way does not always have to be positive. In fact, constant positivity is toxic. We need balance. There is good and bad in this world. There is positivity and negativity. Up and down. Yin and yang. Embrace that balance. Just ensure that the negative beliefs you hold support your growth and can eventually be empowering rather than hindering. When that happens, you develop a rational belief system.

One of the most attractive benefits of CBT is that it can be effective in a short span of time. It is not a magical cure. However, it sets the basis for developing more positive thinking patterns that enlighten and empower. This effectiveness is not limited to one area. It helps reshape many maladaptive behaviors.

In addition to generalized anxiety disorder and depression, the wide range of conditions that can be treated using CBT include:

- Panic attacks
- Obsessive-compulsive disorder

- Personality disorders
- Eating disorders
- Anger management
- Phobias
- Grief or loss
- Sleep disorders like insomnia
- Low self-esteem
- Stress management

CBT also helps with coping with conditions outside the mental health sphere, like:

- Chronic pain
- Serious illness
- Relationship problems like divorce and breakups

Online sessions are just as effective as face-to-face interactions with a therapist.

CBT is also one of the more affordable types of talk therapy. Prices vary based on factors like location and individual therapists. Shop around your area to note the price range.

Sometimes medication is necessary to treat the symptoms of psychiatric issues because of their severity. These medications are known as psychotropic drugs. Examples include antidepressants and antipsychotics. Anxiolytics are used particularly to treat anxiety symptoms as well as insomnia. Hypnotics also aid with sleep disorders. Mood stabilizers help treat bipolar disorders and other mood disorders.

Stimulants are an example that is used to treat ADHD and sleep disorders. These medications affect how your mind works. As such, they alter your emotions and so, your behavior. This is caused by the medications changing the balance of neurotransmitters in the brain. Discuss whether or not such medication is right for your teen with your doctor. If they are taken off the table, then CBT is a great means of treatment.

To summarize, the benefits of CBT include:

- Allowing the development of healthier thinking patterns by creating awareness of negative and unrealistic thinking that brings down your mood and energy.
- Is effective in the short term.
- Is effective for several maladaptive behaviors.
- Online sessions are just as effective as in-person sessions.
- Being a more affordable type of talk therapy.
- Being useful to people who do not require psychotropic medications.

Before we move on to specific CBT techniques, it must be stated that the absence of anxiety is not the mark of positive results from this approach. Instead, success is based on developing the ability to cope with anxiety. The coping skills developed through cognitive behavioral therapy are meant to help your teen not only in the present but also in the future. These skills are also meant to help the entire family cope. These skills are developed in a relatively short time—

typically 3 to 4 months. The need for the therapist's aid can be phased as the teen and the family understand and know how to implement these skills. Improvement will not depend on sessions with the therapist then. This is one of the most powerful advantages that CBT allows anxious teens and their families — the ability to maintain the gains seen from formal therapy sessions even after treatment has ceased. When weighed against the monetary cost of CBT sessions, the potential benefits are enormous. A <u>Verywell Mind's Cost of Therapy Survey</u> highlighted how Americans felt about the financial investment in therapy.

The results were as follows:

- 80% support therapy as a good investment.
- 91% are satisfied with the quality of therapy they receive.
- 84% are satisfied with their progress toward meeting their mental health goals.

The results do not lie. As such, I implore you to seriously consider taking on the temporary cost of CBT sessions with a therapist to help your teen combat anxiety.

If you are still skeptical about how CBT can help your teen, I understand. Perhaps the following evidence supporting its effectiveness with adolescents will ease your mind.

CBT is found to be the best treatment for dealing with eating disorders. CBT is recommended as the primary treatment for adults who suffer from bulimia nervosa and binge eating disorder by the UK's National Institute for Health and Care Excellence (NICE). A study released in 2014 showed that 20 sessions of CBT were a more effective treatment for women with bulimia nervosa compared to weekly sessions of psychoanalytic psychotherapy. Seventy patients were assigned to either group randomly. The CBT session lasted 5 months, and after this time, 42% of these patients had stopped purging and binge eating, while only 6% of the patients from the psychoanalytic groups had seen the same progress. The psychoanalytic therapy was completed in 2 years. After this time, 15% of this group was symptom-free, while 44% of the CBT group had the same result.

CBT has also shown great effectiveness in treating sleep disorders like insomnia. It even helps people who have general medical conditions that interrupt healthy sleep hygiene like mood disorders such as depression and sufferers of chronic pain. A 2018 meta-analysis highlighting over 40 studies showed that CBT helps alleviate the symptoms of anxiety and anxiety-related disorders. The relationship between a teen and the therapist imparting the treatment is paramount. Adolescence is a turbulent time for teens. During this time, many distance themselves from their parents and siblings as they look for value in relationships outside of their family. The relationship between an anxious teen and therapist helps take up the slack that is likely damaging the teen's well-being because of this distance. The therapist helps the teen process stressors in their life. This is necessary as the teen is in a phase of identity development. CBT has shown a success rate between 60% and 80% in youth. This number goes up when the treatment is combined with psychotropic medication. A one-size-fits-all approach to talk therapy will never be successful, as every teen has different needs. Research supports the tailored approach used with CBT as one of the major factors that help create these extraordinary outcomes.

Expected CBT Outcomes

The contribution of the past is certainly relevant. However, CBT focuses on providing your teen with the tools necessary for dealing with the problems they face today. Each anxious teen faces a particular set of problems that magnify their anxious thoughts and so, the wonderful thing about CBT is that the techniques can be customized to address those specific issues.

CBT techniques are used to accomplish the following:

Identify Negative Thoughts

Negative thinking is often a manifestation of irrational core beliefs. As such, negative thinking is a pathway for developing maladaptive behaviors. Connecting thoughts with feelings and triggers is difficult, especially if struggles come from introspection. However, taking that hard road leads to self-discovery. That insight is a must for effective results from CBT.

Practice New Skills

We all use coping mechanisms to get through hard times in life. Some of these coping habits are not healthy and even cause disruptions in our lives. CBT provides skills that develop healthier coping mechanisms. For example, someone with a substance use disorder may have previously avoided social situations that pose a potential trigger to relapses as a coping mechanism. A new, more beneficial coping skill may be to start by attending social events where a support network is present or only attending events where they can be distracted with activities they find enjoyable.

Set Goals

Goals give us direction. They are personal compasses, pointing to our North Star throughout the days of our lives. They fuel us with purpose. They help us get back on our feet when we falter. They allow us to act in both the short term and in the long haul. They are an important component of overcoming any mental issue. The mess of thoughts swirling in your anxious teen's head makes it difficult to set such goals. But with the help of a therapist, **SMART** (**S**pecific, **M**easurable, **A**ttainable, **R**elevant, **T**ime-based) goals can be developed. With that compass firmly in hand, your teen can focus on the process of reaching the desired outcome.

Problem-Solve

Some people say that if it is not one problem, it is another. But a more realistic take is if it is not one problem, it is several others. Problems (big and small) are a natural part of human life, and they can be a source of great stress. Since we can't prevent problems from happening, a needed life skill is problem-solving. What many fail to realize is that problems do not exist just to give us headaches. Within problems exist opportunities for better control in the future. Problem-solving is the tool that enables the exploitation of such opportunities. Problem-solving gives you a sense of control. It, therefore, not only reduces the negative psychological impact of dealing with problems but also helps minimize any physical illnesses that are associated.

CBT teaches the 5 steps of problem-solving:

1. Identify the problem.
2. Create a list of possible solutions for eliminating the problem.
3. Gauge the strengths and weaknesses of each possible solution.
4. Select the solution with the greatest strength and least number of weaknesses to implement.
5. Implement the solution.

Reaching step 5 is not an automatic deduction that the process is complete. Sometimes, the solution does not solve the problem. Luckily, you can use another solution from the list generated in step 2. This process is repeatable. If you have exhausted the list, go back to the drawing board, or seek help from others.

The most important benefit of problem-solving is that it teaches your teen not to be a victim of stressors. It teaches youngsters that they can actively make their life better through their efforts, even when negative thinking pushes the idea that this problem can't be overcome. It shows that action is often better than reaction. This CBT outcome gives a great foundation for dealing with problems throughout their lifetime.

Self-Monitor

Also called diary work, self-monitoring is the skill of tracking behaviors, experiences, and symptoms as they happen over time. For example, a person with an eating disorder may track their eating habits along with their thoughts and feelings whenever they eat over a few months. A depressed person may collect data about the particulars of the situation when their mood feels particularly low. Your anxious teen may be asked to note the events that led up to an anxiety attack from the time of one session with the therapist to another. These records are shared with the therapist during the sessions so treatment can be fine-tuned to suit that individual best.

CBT Techniques

To achieve the outcomes listed above, the most used CBT techniques utilized are:

Journaling

There is something about putting pen to paper that has a way of getting a person in touch with their thoughts. Journaling is also a way of tracking your progress in developing new thought patterns and new behaviors from one CBT session to the next.

Nightmare exposure and rescripting

Like interoceptive exposure (discussed below), this technique is helpful for sufferers of nightmares. Experiencing mental ordeals brings up certain emotions. This exposure strategy deliberately subjects the patient to the associated emotion. The therapist and the patient work together to develop a new image to accompany that emotion. By extension, new responses can also be developed.

Relaxed breathing

Encouraging mindfulness, this technique can be elevated with the use of guided and unguided imagery, scripts, audio recordings, and more to induce relaxation through breath. Anxiety symptoms are often perpetuated through shallow, rapid breathing. Deliberately pacing your breath to one that is regular and deep signals the mind to relax. This CBT technique supports a range of issues and helps stimulate focus and calm.

Progressive muscle relaxation

Reminiscent of a body scan, this mindfulness technique is about becoming aware of tension in each muscle group in the body and deliberately relaxing one at a time until the entire body reaches a state of relaxation. The patient can be guided through this with their own mind or with the help of YouTube videos and audio scripts. Progressive muscle relaxation is particularly useful for gaining focus and calming nerves.

Deciphering cognitive distortions

The first step to becoming untangled from cognitive distortions is awareness. Your teen is taught to identify and challenge automatic thoughts that hinder them.

Playing the script until the end

In the head of an anxious person, the worst-case scenario will always play out. One way to combat such catastrophic thinking is to role-play. Instead of trying to interrupt these thoughts, play them out so that your teen can see potential solutions to these problems. We used to do this with our daughter when she was a youngster. She had developed a lot of anxieties, one of them being traveling through airport security. This fear arose because she got stopped once with a baby doll full of water. She was terrified and did not know what was going to happen when she was stopped. So, whenever we had to fly, which was often due to family living out of state, we would walk through the worst-case scenario. What if she got stopped by TSA with something she wasn't supposed to have? They would take it from her, and she would move on through security. We continued to play this "game" when other anxiety-producing scenarios arose. Fear and anxiety are reduced when your child sees that these are problems that can be dealt with.

This improves problem-solving skills, but it also has additional benefits, such as:

- Improving communication skills.
- Increasing self-confidence and esteem.
- Practicing assertiveness.
- Practicing and improving social skills.
- Improving feelings of coping.

Cognitive restructuring

This technique forces a long, hard look at negative thought patterns. Is it that your teen overgeneralizes? Or blame others? Does your teen display emotional reasoning or lean toward a fallacy of fairness? Perhaps your teen has a black-and-white way of viewing things. These cognitive distortions have a way of becoming self-fulfilling prophecies, empowering negative thoughts. Creating awareness of them is the first step. After they have been detected, your therapist can teach your teen to reframe these thoughts, so they become more productive and positive.

Interoceptive exposure

This technique is intended to treat anxiety and panic by exposing the sufferer to bodily sensations that incite a fearful response. Inciting this response is about exposing the irrational beliefs associated with those bodily sensations. Awareness is developed as the sensation is maintained and not avoided. Herein lies the opportunity for a new sensation association to develop. The patient ultimately sees that even though symptoms of panic are uncomfortable, ultimately, they are not dangerous. Panic can then be controlled.

Exposure and response prevention

Especially effective in OCD cases, this technique is about being subjected to the trigger that normally incites compulsive behavior. The goal is to refrain from that compulsive behavior. This will not happen immediately, but over time the controlled exposure is meant to develop resistance to that automatic behavior. In time, a mindful response will be developed.

It is common to combine this technique with journaling to delve into what emotions are elicited by that exposure. We will discuss this in-depth in the following chapter.

More CBT Exercises

You can never have too many CBT tools and processes to fall back on.

Here are a few more exercises that can be quite effective:

Reframing negative thoughts

Reframing thinking patterns is about challenging negative thoughts and their founding beliefs by first recognizing the cognitive distortions and then actively working to change them to adopt a more realistic and positive view. Reframing negative thought patterns helps your teen feel more optimistic. The adolescent gains the ability to bounce back from stress more easily.

Reframing negative thoughts is not to be confused with cognitive restructuring. Cognitive restructuring is used in collaboration with a therapist to become aware of and replace maladaptive thoughts. Reframing can be used in therapy or on its own so that a person adjusts their mindset to focus more on positive thoughts. The expectation is that this person replaces unrealistic and excessively high expectations with those that are more realistic.

A teen may feel sad that he or she got 80% on a quiz rather than the full score they wanted. They were working to improve their grades after a lack of focus meant a few failing grades the semester before. Reframing teaches them to change how they view the situation. This teenager can focus on the positive, like earning a mark well above the passing grade — an improvement over the results from the past.

Here's a useful practice that helps your teen reframe negative thoughts . . . Get into the habit of noticing negative thoughts by using technology. Have your teenager set reminders on their phone to check in on themselves. They should stop everything that they are doing when these reminders sound and actively think about at 3 least positive things around them.

Worry journaling

Journaling with the specific purpose of purging your teenager of worries and stress helps lean into uncomfortable emotions so they can be dissected. This type of journaling allows the teen to separate themselves from the troubling emotions and actively return to the present. It can also serve as a gauge to determine how factors like hormonal changes, exercise, diet, and more influence stress and anxiety levels.

Social role-playing

Particularly useful for teens with social anxiety, this practice allows teens to engage in social situations that cause them unease. It allows for exploring various scenarios so that they feel better prepared when they happen in real life. It also empowers the teen to stand their ground, implement and enforce boundaries, and use their voice confidently.

Mindfulness meditation

Mindful meditation was discussed in depth in Chapter 2 but let's take a brief look at how it fits into CBT. Mindfulness meditation is particularly useful between therapy sessions as it helps patients become grounded in the moment, especially during moments of stress. It helps them disengage from rumination and obsession caused by hindering automatic thoughts.

CBT Techniques with Worksheets

Worksheets are a great way of guiding your teen through the CBT process. Such worksheets may be used during treatment with the therapist or with a hands-on approach from a loving family member like yourself.

A few worksheets I recommend trying are:

Fact checking worksheet

It is difficult to recognize irrational thoughts as untrue when they are so loud and demand all the attention, but the fact-checking worksheet below gives your teen the ability to decipher which thoughts have merit and which do not. This is where we ask the question: "Is this a fact or a feeling?" I have found this very helpful personally when I am having illogical thoughts, as well as helping my daughter when she is struggling. Consider this as you fill out the worksheet.

At the top of this worksheet, an important fact is stated:

Thoughts are not facts.

This true statement needs to be instilled within your teen. It will not be easy, especially when cognitive distortions invoke intense emotions. However, filling out this worksheet can help your teen come to that realization sooner. The worksheet includes 15 statements that your teen must decide whether or not they should be ticked as fact or opinion. I think it is helpful to think of it as "fact or feeling?"

Statements include:

- I'm dumb.
- I failed the exam.
- I'm selfish.
- I dislike my job.

There are no trick answers to these statements. The correct answers for the statement above follow a pattern that looks like this: opinion, fact, opinion, fact.

The simple motive behind this worksheet is to show the youth that most emotionally charged thoughts do not carry weight as objective truths. The teen must be taught to recognize the difference between opinion and fact to effectively challenge negative thinking and uplift their opinion of themselves.

Fact Checking Thoughts Worksheet

The *fact Checking Thoughts* worksheet helps clients to recognise that their thoughts are not necessarily true. The key take-home message from this worksheet is:

Thoughts are not facts.

It can be difficult to accept the idea that thoughts are not facts at first especially when we are in the throes of an emotion. However, completing this worksheet will help you come to this realisation.

The worksheet contains 15 statements that the client must decide are either fact or opinion. These statements include:

- "I'm not good enough"
- "I failed the test"
- "This will be a disaster"
- "I'm overweight"

Note, there is a correct answer for each statement (In case you're wondering, the right answers for the statements above are as follows: opinion, fact opinion, fact).

This simple exercise can help clients see that while we have lots of emotionally charged thoughts, they are not all absolute truths. Recognising the difference between fact and opinion can assist us in challenging the dysfunctional or harmful opinions we have about ourselves and others.

Fact Checking Thoughts Worksheet
Worksheet

We tend to believe each and every thought we have is true; however, thoughts are not facts. While some thoughts we have may be factual (e.g. *"I failed the test"*), others may not (e.g., *"I am dumb"*).

These non-factual thoughts are *opinions*. This worksheet is designed to help you practice differentiating between factual thoughts and opinions (i.e., thoughts that are not necessarily fact).

Statement	Fact	Opinion
I'm dumb	☐	☐
I'm unattractive	☐	☐
I failed the exam	☐	☐
I have no friends	☐	☐
Nobody likes me	☐	☐
I'm a selfish person	☐	☐
This will be a disaster	☐	☐
I will fail this test	☐	☐
I'm not good enough	☐	☐
I'm overweight	☐	☐
I am single	☐	☐
I will be single forever	☐	☐
My family is disappointed in me	☐	☐
I dislike my job	☐	☐
I'm not good at my job	☐	☐

Thought records worksheet

Thought records help discern when and why negative thoughts pop up. The more your teen learns about these automatic thoughts, the easier they are to address and reframe. Thought records test the validity of thoughts by gathering and evaluating evidence that supports them as factual or not.

For example, the belief may be this: *My friend thinks I'm a bad friend.* Seeming evidence to support this belief may be that this friend didn't pick up the phone the last time you called, or she canceled the plans you both made at the last minute. Evidence against this belief may be that she called back after not answering the phone, and she invited you to a party next week.

If she thought I was a bad friend, she probably wouldn't have invited me. Therefore, it stands to reason that the initial thought is likely irrational. Whether evidence for and against the thought is gathered, the goal is to come up with more balanced thoughts, such as: *My friend is busy and has other friends, so she can't always answer the phone when I call. Being understanding of this allows me to be a good friend.* When irrational thoughts are warded off with logic, they can be replaced with balanced, rational thoughts such as this.

Thought Record Worksheet

The Thought Record worksheet provides a template for clients to monitor their thoughts and emotions, evaluate their thinking, and explore adaptive responding. It is particularly helpful for those clients who are experiencing negative or dysfunctional thoughts and feelings.

The worksheet has 7 steps:

1. On the far left column, there is space to write down the date and time a dysfunctional thought arose.
2. The second column is where the situation is listed. Instruct the client to describe - in detail - the event that led up to the dysfunctional thought.
3. The third column is for the automatic thought. This is where the dysfunctional automatic thought is recorded, along with a rating of belief in the thought on a scale from 0% to 100%.
4. The next column is where the emotion(s) elicited by this thought are listed also with a rating of intensity on a scale from 0% to 100%.
5. The fifth column is where the client will identify which cognitive distortion(s) they are experiencing with regards to this specific dysfunctional thought, such as all-or-nothing thinking, filtering, jumping to conclusions, etc.
6. The second to last column is for the user to write down alternative thoughts, more positive and functional thoughts that can replace the negative one.
7. Finally, the last column is for the user to write down the outcome of this exercise. Were you able to confront the dysfunctional thought? Did you write down a convincing alternative thought? Did your belief in the thought and/or the intensity of your emotion(s) decrease?

Lillian Middleton

Thought Record
Worksheet

Directions: When you notice your mood drop, take a moment to notice what thoughts are passing through your mind, and then jot these down in the Automatic Thoughts column. Then, complete the rest of the row (i.e., date & time, situation, and so on).

Date & time	Situation	Automatic thought(s)	Emotion(s)	Alternative thought(s)	Outcome
	What were you doing?	What exactly were you thinking at the time? And how much did you believe each thought (0-100%)?	How did you feel at the time? And how intense was the emotion (0-100%)?	What evidence is there that the automatic thought is true? Is there an alternative explanation?	How much do you believe in the original automatic thought now (0-100%)? How do you feel now (0-100%)? What can you do now?

Graded exposure worksheet

This technique may sound frightening, but it is truly simple and straightforward. Graded exposure is about addressing avoidance of objects, activities, or situations that cause anxiety. For example, a person with social anxiety might typically avoid going out with friends or making phone calls. The graded exposure worksheet prompts the patient to list the situations that would normally be avoided. These are noted in a hierarchy.

The points listed are then rated based on how distressing the patient finds them. The scale goes from 1 to 10. For a sufferer of social anxiety, going out with friends may be more troubling than making a phone call, and it will rank closer to 10, while the phone call may be closer to 1 with a 3 or 4 rating.

These rated situations will then be ranked based on the level of distress they cause. The patient has a visual representation of the situations they normally avoid. This allows for recognizing the biggest obstacles they face. Now comes the decision of which difficult situations they would like to address and in what order. It is probably best to start your teen off on the least upsetting item to build confidence that they can handle this. Gradually work up to items with more distressing rates.

Graded Exposure Worksheet

Graded Exposure is a CBT technique that is designed to help people confront and overcome their fears. When people are fearful of something, they tend to avoid it

While this avoidance may help in reducing feelings of fear in the short term, over the long term rt can make the fear even worse.

Graded exposure involves creating a safe environment in which clients can become 'exposed* to the things they fear and avoid. The exposure to the feared objects, activities or situations in a safe environment helps reduce fear and decrease avoidance.

The Graded Exposure worksheet includes 4 steps:

1. **Make a list of feared situations that you tend to avoid.** For example, someone with social anxiety may typically avoid making a phone call or asking someone on a date.

2. **Rate each item** according to how distressed you would feel if you encountered that situation, on a scale from 0 to 100% (0 = not at all distressed and 100 = extremely distressed). For the person suffering with severe social anxiety, asking someone on a date may be rated a 10 on the scale, while making a phone call instead might be rated closer to a 3 or 4.

3. **Rank items from most-feared** (i.e.. highest distress rating) at the top of the staircase to least feared (i.e., lowest distress rating) at the bottom of the staircase.

4. **The staircase can now be used to guide a process of the graded exposure.** Clients can be guided to start exposing themselves to the least-feared items, building up as more confidence is gained. Key principles of exposure should be discussed (e.g. stay in situation without escaping, attempt multiple repeats of each exposure to encourage extinction).

Graded Exposure Worksheet

Worksheet

Construct a staircase with situations you tend to avoid because of fear or anxiety, with most-feared items at the top and least-feared items at the bottom. Rate each item according to how distressed you would feel if you encountered that situation, on a scale from 0 to 10 (0 = not at all distressed and 10 = extremely distressed).

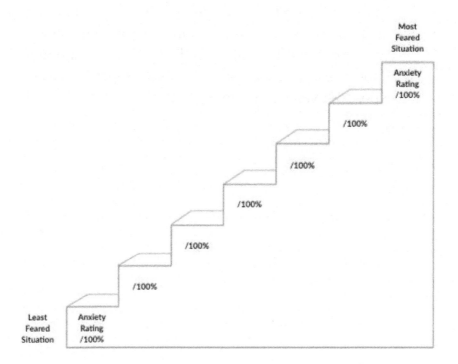

Potential Challenges of CBT

CBT is not a perfect therapy. No therapy is.

As such, a few possible challenges you may encounter with CBT therapy are:

- Change can be hard to handle. Even though a CBT patient recognizes irrational and unhealthy thoughts, awareness alone is not enough to facilitate the process of altering them into more rational and healthy thinking patterns.

- The patient must be willing to change to see positive results. The effectiveness of CBT is reliant on how willing and ready a patient is to spend the time and effort needed to analyze their thoughts and feelings. This person must do the homework assigned by the therapist. Even though it is difficult when the homework places the patients face-to-face with uncomfortable thoughts and feelings, it is necessary to get in touch with those internal conditions to have a positive outward impact on behavior.

- The structure of CBT may be intimidating. Unlike psychoanalytic therapy, CBT does not focus on the underlying issues that may cause resistance to change. The focus is here and now, and this structure may discourage some patients, especially as the therapist has an instructional role.

- Progress is not instantaneous. Rather, progress with CBT is often gradual as it helps a person change behavior in incremental steps. Progressively working toward large goals with small action steps makes the process less daunting and the goals easier to accomplish overall. However, the lack of instant gratification puts some people off the therapy.

Getting Started with CBT

The information outlined in this chapter was written to give you an overview of what CBT is and how it might potentially benefit your teenager who struggles with anxiety.

If you decide that this is worth further consideration, the steps for getting started are:

1. Locate a cognitive-behavioral therapist in your area. There are several routes that you can take to arrive at this. You may consult with your doctor or call (800)253-0167, which is the number for the National Association of Cognitive-Behavioral Therapists. They will be able to let you know if there is a certified therapist in your area. Alternatively, you can seek the right person to talk your teen through symptoms by contacting the local mental health services, your school counselor, or the community health center.

2. Consider whether face-to-face or online therapy works best for you and your teen.

3. Contact your health insurance to note whether CBT is covered. If it is, discover how many sessions per year are covered.

4. Expect the initial experience to be similar to a doctor's appointment, with much paperwork to be filled out.

5. Typical information required includes:

    - Insurance details.
    - Medical history.
    - Any current medications being used.

- A questionnaire about symptoms suffered.
- HIPAA forms.
- A therapist-patient service agreement.

6. Prepare yourself and your teen to answer several questions, such as:
    - What made you seek out therapy.
    - The symptoms experienced.
    - Your teen's history of anxiety.
    - The current living situation.
    - Your child's medical history and any medications they are taking.

I hope this chapter has stirred up your curiosity about CBT, as we will continue the discussion with an in-depth look at the therapy in the next chapter.

CHAPTER 6
CBT II: Face Your Fears

Exposure therapy is an important aspect of treating anxiety with CBT. In particular, we will be discussing prolonged exposure (PE), which teaches people how to approach trauma-related feelings, situations, and memories in a step-by-step process that ultimately leads to freedom from the negative effects they cause. Anxiety makes us want to avoid unpleasant things because, even buried deep within our psyche, they cause us to become encapsulated by fear. PTSD (post-traumatic stress disorder) is a mental condition that arises due to experiencing a terrifying event. This event could be experienced personally or witnessed. It could arise from a person's perception of what is going on.

Typical symptoms of PTSD include:

- Uncontrollable thoughts and troubling memories relating to the event.
- Flashbacks.
- Nightmares and unsettling dreams about the event.
- Severe anxiety and emotional distress.

Your teen's anxiety could be caused by PTSD. We often liken PTSD to the hardships that military personnel suffer after having been in battle. The clear signs are the violent nightmares and flashbacks that are enfeebling. However, this typical example does not show the entire picture. Many reasons exist for developing PTSD. Having lived through a disaster like a flood or a car crash. Having witnessed or been part of an incident where someone was badly injured or killed. Being the victim of a violent crime or physical abuse. Teens develop PTSD from bad home situations, being bullied, natural disasters, and neighborhood violence. Indeed, the recent COVID-19 pandemic has left more than a few people, including teenagers, traumatized. Most of the time, PTSD is not obvious. It worms its way through your teen's life in subtle ways that seem small but have a huge impact on functioning and daily life. It is sad to say but, often, the signs go unnoticed and so, they go untreated. PTSD impacts mood and reactions because your teen is operating in the fight or flight mode almost 24/7. Their feelings of anxiety lead to angry outbursts and irritability. Their self-esteem drops to an all-time low, and they feel ashamed. They blame themselves for their feelings and feel less than other people around them. They lose interest in the things they once enjoyed. They feel detached from the people they care about and those who care about them. Negative thoughts intrude, and the outlook on the future becomes bleak and hopeless. They engage in self-destructive behaviors and self-sabotage.

Prolonged exposure is a cognitive behavioral therapy approach that can help your teen face the things they fear. Before we move into the specifics of how to do that, it is important to note that in PE, your teen is NOT exposed to the traumatizing event. Instead, your teen is exposed to the

MEMORY. The memory of something that has already happened and is in the past. It is not dangerous and cannot hurt your loved one. Patients of PE ultimately learn that the memories and the situations and feelings that trigger them cannot hurt them and do not need to be avoided.

More about PE

This mental health treatment allows people to confront their fears in a safe, systematic way. The goal of PE is to reduce anxiety so the person can finally stop avoiding situations that invoke painful memories. This will improve their quality of life instead of focusing on avoidance. Most people with PTSD believe they think about their trauma all the time, but in reality, when they are at risk of thinking about the trauma, they avoid it or distract themselves. Avoidance only reinforces fear, though. If the trauma is like bad food, they spit it out. It doesn't work for them in the long term. PE is about "digesting" the trauma slowly and methodically, so it is not upsetting every day. PE finally confronts what they have tried so hard to avoid, so this person sees a tremendous decrease in the symptoms of PTSD. The patient can finally look past that event to live life without holding on to the umbrella fear has convinced them is a safe harbor. PE is not just used to treat PTSD.

It is also a proposed treatment for other mental health conditions, such as:

- Specific phobias
- Panic disorder
- Obsessive-compulsive disorder

- Social anxiety disorder
- Generalized anxiety disorder

This approach does indeed sound great on paper. But how effective is prolonged exposure in adolescents? Let's explore this now. Developed by Edna Foa, Ph.D., Director of the Center for the Treatment and Study of Anxiety at the University of Pennsylvania, prolonged exposure has been validated by more than two decades of research. The treatment is based on cognitive behavioral principles. As such, it can be adapted to fit individual needs.

The specific purpose is to help patients finally healthily process traumatic events so that the associated psychological disturbances can be reduced. Various controlled studies have shown its effectiveness in reducing the symptoms of chronic anger, depression, PTSD, and anxiety in trauma patients. Mental health practitioners in and out of the United States currently use cognitive behavioral therapy to treat patients suffering from trauma that results due to incidents such as assault, child abuse, motor vehicle accidents, disasters, rape, and more. It has even been shown to be effective in treating substance use disorders when blended with substance use treatment.

Exposure and Response Prevention for Treatment of OCD

In the 1990s, several studies highlighted the effectiveness of CBT on kids and teens with OCD. In particular, a type of CBT called exposure and response prevention (ERP) was used. The success rate in these studies ranged between 65% and 80%.

This rate was almost parallel with the success rate experienced when the treatment was used on adults.

This success was not likened to luck. It was obtained because ERP addressed the underlying behaviors that make OCD what it is.

OCD is characterized by two features:

1. Compulsive behaviors (also called rituals).
2. Avoidant behavior that provides temporary relief from the stress of anxiety.

Let's use an example to illustrate. Thirteen-year-old Cassandra worries about diseases and feels contaminated if she flushes the toilet with her hands. So, she flushes with her foot, thus lessening her anxiety surrounding the situation. Her anxiety symptoms are lessened by the behavior . . . That is how it seems on the surface. Truth be told, the teen's anxiety and, thus, her OCD is exacerbated by her action. Performing this "ritual" prevents her from learning that her obsession with contamination and disease is improbable, and the ritual is unhelpful. It makes her brain think there is truth to her fear when there is no solid basis for it. By continuing to perform the ritual, she is not challenging the mistaken beliefs, which is the true way of lessening her anxiety. The reality is that her anxiety increases over time due to repeated performance of compulsions rather than letting nature take its course or using coping skills to reduce anxiety.

ERP would serve Cassandra (and others like her) well. It teaches youth with OCD not to give in to compulsive and avoidant behavior, so they can face their fears. Going toe-to-toe with these horrors allows for challenging them. It allows for questions and analysis. When a light is shined on them, more often than not, the truth is realized—these fears reside in the head and nowhere else. Logic and reasoning lead the way to the anxiety experienced, subsiding through the process called habituation. Simply put, habituation is a psychological process of "getting used to it." Repeated exposure to a trigger leads to a decreased response to it. The principle is that OCD patients like Cassandra learn to ignore the trigger due to repeated exposure. She gets used to it by flushing the toilet with her hands and then going through the process of thorough (but not extended) handwashing.

Using PE to Treat PTSD in Adolescents

Usually, prolonged exposure is done with the guidance of a licensed therapist over 3 months through weekly individual sessions. The patient attends 8 to 15 sessions in total. Originally, 12 sessions, each 90 minutes in length, were the recommendation for effectiveness. However, as advances have been made in the therapy, 60- to 120-minute sessions have become the norm so that sufficient processing of trauma can be experienced during that period.

To start, therapists provide patients with an overview of what to expect and spend time understanding the patient's past trauma. Therapists will also engage in psychoeducation so the patient has a greater understanding of their condition and how they will proceed. It will also provide general techniques for managing anxiety, such as deep breathing.

Only then will exposure begin.

Understandably, for most patients, exposure induces anxiety. Therefore, it is such a necessary step that the therapist develops a good relationship with the patient so that they can know that they are in a safe space when encountering these triggers.

The two types of prolonged exposure commonly used to neutralize traumatizing memories are:

- Imaginal exposure
- In vivo exposure

Imaginal exposure

The patient is guided by the therapist to describe the distressing event in detail. This is done in the present tense so that the patient can process the emotions they felt at that time. The retelling is recorded so the patient can listen in between sessions and more deeply process the emotions while practicing coping mechanisms such as breathing techniques.

In vivo exposure

Confrontation of the feared object or situation is done by developing a list of items that remind the patient of the traumatic experience. Such reminders are typically everyday things. For example, a survivor of a car crash may be reminded of that event by video games featuring cars, walking along the roadside, or even sitting in a car.

After this list has been developed, along with the guidance of the PE therapist, the patient will do exposure exercises that typically begin with mental imagery of the feared object or situation. The therapist will provide support along with coping mechanisms during such time.

When the patient is ready to progress, exposure to real-life experiences and situations that pose as a trigger is the next step. Therefore, the survivor of the vehicular accident, who may be afraid of cars, may gain exposure by sitting in a car for a few minutes to a few hours.

The patient is encouraged to challenge themselves and the limits fear has imposed on them. Prolonged exposure to triggers is difficult, but the treatment is designed so that it is not *too* difficult. Success is the aim. The patient and the therapists have continuous conversations about the patient's comfort level to prevent overwhelm. The patient is not forced to do anything they are not ready to do.

Neither of these types of prolonged exposure is superior to the other. They are often used in conjunction with each other. The pace at which they are utilized is ruled by the patient's response.

Other types of prolonged exposure that you may encounter include:

- Applied muscle tension – Similar to in vivo exposure, this approach incorporates muscle tension exercises and is particularly helpful to people who tend to pass out due to a phobia surrounding blood.
- Systematic desensitization – Exposure to increasing levels of anxiety-inducing triggers while the patient practices relaxation techniques in an effort to reduce anxiety toward the stimulus.
- Virtual reality exposure – The use of computer programs to simulate objects or situations that involve fear so that the patient interacts with the trigger in a virtual environment.

After exposure, the conclusion of the therapy includes exercises that serve to prevent relapse.

To be clear, PE is done in four phases:

1. Pre-treatment preparation
2. Psychoeducation and treatment planning
3. Exposure
4. Relapse prevention and conclusion of treatment

As mentioned before, PE is designed to be amended to fit the specific needs of individual patients. Therefore, it is highly appropriate to meet the developmental concerns and needs of teenagers. It will involve exercises that are appropriate for the age level as well as family intervention. Homework assignments will be given in between sessions that allow the teenager to confront people, objects, or situations they have been avoiding, not to be reminded of the trauma with in vivo exposure. This homework may come in the form of imaginal exposure, where they are tasked with listening to the audio recordings of their recollection of the traumatic experience.

Obstacles to Exposure Treatment

One of the most common challenges experienced when imparting any form of exposure therapy for teens is the avoidance of homework. Teachers of all grade levels in middle and high school complain about students not doing homework. Unfortunately, most teens carry that noncompliance over to exposure therapy. The assignments between sessions with the therapist are important for progress. To get a successful outcome, it must be done.

Noncompliance is typical and to be expected. Your teen is not just being rebellious. They are exhibiting avoidant behavior. If and when this issue arises, confront it immediately and directly without shaming or judgment. The therapist will address this at the beginning of the session. Noncompliance is not a reason to postpone sessions or the agenda to be accomplished during each session.

Limited resources also rear their head as a challenge. Most people with OCD below the age of 18 years old do not receive ERP because there is a limited number of professionals who specialize in the expertise. This age group possesses unique developmental needs. The therapist needs to be well-versed in working with children and adolescents because calming this age group is a must, as facing fears can seem like an insurmountable task. Not only must the therapist guide the youth through exposure, but the therapist must also prepare the teen or child for that exposure. Failure to do so is likely to lead to the teen withdrawing from exposure or maybe outright refusing to participate.

For therapy to work, the therapist must possess knowledge and experience in using age-appropriate techniques that make the teen comfortable. The therapist must also appreciate the importance of family involvement and how to integrate that into the therapy. Games have always been a go-to when working with minors, but metaphors and analogies open up a whole new world when relating to teens and younger age groups. It helps them understand complicated concepts like how exposure and habituation work. The more they understand, the easier it is to get them on board with the sessions. They recognize that you respect their intellect and so elicit their cooperation. They are more willing to endure and overcome the initial bouts of anxiety that exposure introduces. PE and ERP are collaborative exercises where teens, families, and therapists work together to overcome anxiety.

The Need for a Multifaceted and Adaptable Plan

Any type of exposure therapy is meant to improve the overall quality and well-being of the teenager. It is not just about treating anxiety symptoms, compulsions, obsessions, or even traumatic memories. The foundation of exposure therapy is about removing the doubts and negative thoughts that chip at the teen's mental health and happiness so improvements in overall self-esteem can be made. Only then can the building and rebuilding of family relationships, social skills, academic functioning, and other areas of life be done. While the symptoms of the teen's particular mental health issue are the first area of treatment, it is by no means the last stop.

You must talk to your therapist about developing a plan that ticks off strategic actions that enable this ultimate balance.

CBT is sometimes hard for patients who have "dysfunctional thought patterns." Such thinking leads to assumptions that they are being blamed or are broken in some way. They see the homework as an indication that they aren't good enough. Validating expressive talk therapy alone can make these patients feel overly dependent and worsen symptoms. There is still hope if your teen falls into that category. It is called dialectical behavioral therapy (DBT). This is a type of CBT that guides your teen toward self-acceptance while working toward changing their negative outlook into a more positive one. The next chapter is dedicated to outlining what DBT is and how it might be the answer to your teen's particular issues.

CHAPTER 7

DBT – Acceptance and Change

Dialectical Behavior Therapy (DBT) is a testament that opposite things can both be true as they exist at the same time in history. The word dialectical gives this away. It means "concerned with or acting through opposing forces" or opposite ideas. In this case, a teen with anxiety that has wrecked their outlook on themselves and the world can accept this view as it is, while simultaneously pursuing a truth that pivots in the opposite direction. That truth is to change this interpretation of reality. There is balance in this way of thinking, and that is what DBT is aimed at accomplishing—showing a teen with a skewed mindset that it is okay that this is your current reality while pressing the accelerator to gain the momentum to develop a new way of thinking. This is not an overnight process. It is a journey, and it needs to be accepted that there will be ups and downs, hills and valleys, wins and losses.

What Is DBT?

DBT is a type of CBT. As such, it is psychotherapy. Its effectiveness is based on a solid relationship developed between a patient and a therapist. Their sessions involve lots of deep conversations aimed at highlighting and understanding the patient's thoughts and how these affect their emotions and actions. DBT is best for people who experience highly intense emotions. The sessions focus on teaching them to accept what their current reality is as well as help develop a mindset and the basis for actions that remove self-harming and self-sabotaging behavior so they can experience positive change.

There is much pain and discomfort when negative thoughts have a vice grip on your mind. They sink their talons deep and attempts to pull free lead to deeper hurt. In trying to find relief, people who experience this tend to attempt numbing the pain with nonconstructive coping mechanisms like substance use. We have learned that this only offers temporary solace. The pain only comes back stronger when the effects wear off. DBT teaches the patient to sit with these thoughts instead of trying to be rid of them. The emphasis is not on those thoughts, though. It is about teaching the patient to locate the triggers outside of their mind and then contest those triggers with healthy coping mechanisms and responses. Negative thoughts can seem like big, scary monsters that need to be hidden from, but DBT is tailored toward helping people acknowledge that, yes, they feel pain. Yes, they feel unsettled and unnerved. But that is okay. Those thoughts are only that and cannot hurt you. Acknowledgment is followed by highlighting that this person is safe despite the disquiet. From that foundation, this person can be empowered to choose healthy coping behaviors instead of harmful or impulsive ones.

Who Needs DBT?

Developed in the 1970s, DBT has been scientifically proven to work effectively in random-controlled trials (RCT) in both academic and community spheres since the 1980s.

DBT has helped a wide range of people, such as those suffering from:

- Anxiety
- Depression
- Eating disorders like bulimia and binge eating
- PTSD
- Borderline personality disorder (BPD)
- Substance abuse disorder
- Self-harm
- Suicidal thoughts and behaviors
- Trauma like sexual abuse

Instead of just trying to talk or think through the concerns developed because of the aforementioned issues, the focus of DBT is to change behavioral patterns. Sometimes we feel like we are walking through a world where sticks and stones and other things that will break our bones are continuously being jabbed at us. It doesn't feel like there is time to think or talk things through. There are only impulses and explosive reactions to these intense things that we feel.

Some people feel like there is never an escape from these feelings. Nonetheless, they try to escape the pain the best they know how with coping mechanisms that temporarily remove the hurt. But those coping actions most often only add another weapon against them. DBT teaches patients to walk through this world filled with acceptance because that is the only way you can get to the other side where the pain is not so sharp and the sun shines bright, even if for just moments at a time.

While CBT focuses on feelings, thoughts, and behaviors and how these three elements influence each other, DBT focuses more heavily on learning to accept pain, being more mindful, and regulating emotions to keep from acting out potentially destructive and harmful behaviors.

DBT sessions typically include the following elements:

- Group therapy with 4 modules.
- Patients are taught behavioral skills.
- Individual weekly sessions where the patient meets with a DBT therapist or coach to build on the behavioral skills learned in the group therapy.
- The patient learns to personalize these skills to fit their particular circumstances.
- Phone coaching between sessions to receive guidance about challenging situations currently being faced.

When a patient is better able to regulate their emotions, improve their relationships with other people, and be more mindful, they can transition to standard CBT sessions to address specific negative thought patterns or reoccurring harmful behaviors.

Deciding between CBT or DBT is a matter of noting which therapy shows the most benefit in treating your teen's particular diagnosis and the symptoms related to that disorder. If your teen has not yet received a diagnosis from a psychologist or psychiatrist, consider setting up an appointment to get one. It is only with this verification that you can pursue the best treatment options as well as leverage existing skills and advantages of that treatment.

Often, CBT is best for persons with anxiety and depressive disorders, while DBT is more effective for people with borderline personality disorder or chronic thoughts of suicide. Most people do not fit into a mold, though, and receive more than one diagnosis. As such, elements of both CBT and DBT can be used to manage their symptoms. Therefore, I cannot stress this enough—only a formal diagnosis can help you pave the best path forward using these therapies.

The First Four Core Skills of DBT

There are four core skills developed using DBT:

Mindfulness

This first foundational skill helps patients become grounded in the current moment. They learn to pay attention to what is happening now without overthinking and without judgment. This is a powerful coping tool as it allows acceptance of situations as they are currently, even the pain that is felt. Fighting pain only leads to more suffering. The mindfulness practices taught are grounded in traditional Zen and Buddhism.

Teens are taught to interact with their environment both inside and outside through the five senses of sound, taste, smell, sight, and touch. They develop their powers of observation so that they can describe, without judgment, what their senses tell them. Next, come lessons on how to become fully focused and immersed in the things they are doing through wholehearted participation. Through observation, description, and participation, teens learn to appreciate both simple and complex moments, even those that are challenging.

Emotion Regulation

This skill is about navigating the ups and downs of emotions. It is not about ignoring negative or overwhelming emotions. Instead, it is about developing methods of coping during such times so they can increase their positive experiences. Negative emotions are not the bad guy they are often portrayed as. They are simply a normal part of life and don't have to be and should not be avoided. The teen is taught to acknowledge and let go of negative emotions because holding on to them only leads to them controlling their behaviors. Emotional regulation puts the control in your teen's hands.

Interpersonal Effectiveness

No man is an island. We all need to effectively communicate and interact with other people to live a life that is well-rounded and full. This foundational skill is aimed at developing the tools for managing relationships and interpersonal connections, even those that are multifaceted and have intricate details.

Distress Tolerance

This core skill focuses on increasing patients' tolerance of negative emotions. Instead of becoming overwhelmed and being avoidant, patients are taught to strive for calm in triggering situations. Instead of being led by negative emotions, the aim is to make conscientious decisions about what healthy actions should be taken.

The Fifth Core Skill of DBT

A fifth element is incorporated into adolescent DBT programs. Invented by Dr. Marsha M. Linehan, who struggled with BPD, it is called *Walking the Middle Path*. It was specifically created to cater to the needs of that age group. *Walking the Middle Path* is about replacing either-or thinking with a mindset of both-and. It is about compromise and finding the middle ground. Often, persons with dysfunctional thinking view life from a black-and-white lens that does not allow any flexibility. *Walking the Middle Path* deconstructs this so the teen learns to value their perspective but also accepts that there may be alternatives that are also valid.

The principle that allows this shift is the teen getting out of a state of being and into a state of doing.

This is facilitated through mindful practices like:

- Accepting, without judgment, how the world is presently with no thought or action to change it.
- Recognizing that situations can be viewed and problems can be solved in more than one way.
- Substantiating your perceptions and experiences.

- Validating the perceptions and experiences of other people.

- Affirming the belief that change is created through action as well as acceptance, understanding, and validation. As such, you have control of your internal world, meaning your thoughts and feelings as well as your external world, meaning your actions and words—no matter what situation you face.

"A life worth living."

Those are the words of Dr. Linehan. The aim of *Walking the Middle Path* is to help adolescents with anxiety disorders, depressive disorders, and other psychological disorders learn practical skills they can rely on at any time to cope with any situation. They learn to effectively process and then manage their emotions, so they do not become overwhelmed and swallowed by them. Why? So they can create a life they believe is *worth living*.

Radical Acceptance

Radical acceptance is considered a cornerstone of DBT. While we have touched on acceptance throughout this chapter, I want to focus on radical acceptance. We will discuss the definition, how to practice it, situations that warrant it and those that do not, and some coping statements to use in this practice.

Radical acceptance has its roots in Buddhism and is based on the idea that anguish emanates from one's attachment to the pain you are feeling rather than precisely from the pain itself. Its definition is the acceptance of a situation that is beyond your control, without judgment. This action serves to reduce the suffering caused by the situation. It is important to note that acceptance of the situation does not imply approval of what is happening, just that you are accepting reality and not disputing it. It is not a passive act, like normal acceptance. You must put conscious thought and effort into it in order to separate yourself from your suffering. Radical acceptance is a form of distress tolerance. Some indications that you or your teen may need to practice radical acceptance are if phrases like this sound familiar: *This is not fair. It shouldn't be like this. I will never get over what happened. Bad things always happen to me.*

According to DBT's founder Marsha Linehan, here are 10 steps to practicing Radical Acceptance:

1. Notice that you are fighting reality (*"it shouldn't be like this"*).

2. Tell yourself that the difficult reality is what it is and cannot be altered (*"what happened, happened"*).

3. Remember that there are reasons for this reality (*"this is how it occurred"*).

4. Rehearse accepting this reality with your whole self (mind, body, and spirit). Utilize accepting self-talk, mindfulness, relaxation, and visualization.

5. Make a list of what you would do if you accepted the reality of the situation and then live life as if you have accepted that reality.

6. Visualize, with your eyes closed, what you do not want to accept and play out scenarios of what would happen if you were to accept the unacceptable.

7. Stay attuned to your body during this time as you determine what reality needs to be accepted.

8. Loss, grief, and sadness may bubble up. That is ok.

9. Recognize that life is worthwhile even in the face of great pain.

10. Create a pro and con list if you find yourself coming up against a wall when trying to attain acceptance.

There are some situations where radical acceptance is not appropriate. Usually, they involve situations that you have an amount of control over. Also, any situation that is dangerous, abusive, or where you are being taken advantage of. In addition, any scenario where you are using acceptance as a crutch not to have to face reality or people pleasing so as not to have to stand up for yourself.

Finally, here are some coping phrases to help you in your practice of radical acceptance:

- *I have no control over the events of the past.*
- *It is not helpful to resist the events of the past.*
- *I only have control over my actions in the present moment.*
- *I will never know the why, but I can accept that it happened.*
- *I can accept the past and still feel joyful.*

If your teen has been through trauma or other negative events in life and you notice them either stuffing down their emotions or acting overly emotional (hard to tell in a teenager sometimes!), then while it won't be easy, radical acceptance might be the step that brings them to peace.

The Ultimate DBT Skill That Can Lift Almost Any Teen's Negative Outlook

A skill taught within the emotional regulation aspect of the DBT program can be a game-changer for your teen. It is called Opposite Action. Human beings are emotional creatures. Emotions move us to respond. Some behaviors get wired into us. This can be a good thing. For example, if we feel thirsty, there is a biological response wired into us that tells us to hydrate and so, the response is to drink water. If we are hungry, we respond to the need to give our bodies fuel by eating.

However, when we respond with impulsive behavior that has potentially harmful or destructive consequences, we need to rewire that response. Opposite Action develops the skill of consciously choosing to respond in the opposite way that has become ingrained.

It is particularly useful for teens who are struggling with:

- Anger management
- Trauma
- Low self-esteem
- Depression
- Anxiety

Teens can use Opposite Action when experiencing a painful emotion that does not fit the context or is not effective at helping a situation currently. Let's say Julia wears a wig due to alopecia. None of her friends are aware of this fact, and she keeps what she calls "her secret shame" hidden. She often gets invited to sleepovers but declines because she knows she would have to let her friends see her without her wig on. Because the thought of herself without her wig causes her to feel shameful with low self-esteem, and this emotion does not fit the facts of the situation and isn't effective, she should do exactly the opposite of what she's tempted to do. She should attend sleepovers with her head held high and confidently take off her wig and show off her beautiful bald head, for there is nothing wrong with having a hair loss disorder. This action will lead to changing emotions, even if the action is not done genuinely in the initial instances.

Opposite Action is not always the right skill suited for a situation. When the emotion does *not* fit the context nor does it effectively help the situation currently, Opposite Action should not be used. If a teenager has shoplifted and feels anxious and guilty the next time he goes into the store, Opposite Action should not be used. These feelings are justified and do not warrant using an Opposite Action. Ignoring feelings of anxiety and guilt and holding his head up high as he waltzes into the store as if innocent, only encourages negative behaviors in the future. Instead, the teenager needs to fess up to his crime and pay the price.

CHAPTER 8

Continuing the Journey

We are coming toward the last page in this book, and the first thing I want to say as we reach this end is congratulations. You are showing remarkable commitment to helping your teenager overcome anxiety by reading this far. You have chosen to set them up for success, which is the most significant step you will ever take to achieve that happy, healthy, balanced child you aspire to see.

The next thing that needs to be said is this — this is not the end of your journey in getting the help your teenager needs. Let this book serve as a catalyst that helps you continuously nourish your mind with the necessary resources they need to succeed. This chapter is short, sweet, and to the point, with a list of strongholds that can help them. The resources listed are not just great for anxious teens but also provide aid for parents of kids with anxiety.

Crisis Phone Numbers

Most kids are glued to a cell phone these days. Along with a number of friends and family programmed into the device, I suggest having several emergency numbers saved. Of course, you should have parents and other people the teen trusts to provide help added to the directory. Being able to reach out for help immediately makes a difference.

This list can include:

- The non-emergency number for the local police department
- **The Crisis Text Line: Text HELLO to 741741**
- **988 Suicide & Crisis Lifeline: Call or text 988** (best for people with suicidal thoughts who need immediate help)
- **Trevor Lifeline for the LGBTQ Community: Call 1-866-488-7386, text START to 678678,** or contact them through their website: https://www.thetrevorproject.org/.

Books

- Mind Over Mood, Second Edition: Change How You Feel by Changing the Way You Think 2nd Edition, Kindle Edition
by Dennis Greenberger, Ph.D. and Christine A. Padesky, Ph.D.
- DBT® Skills Training Handouts and Worksheets, Second Edition
by Marsha M. Linehan.

- The Dialectical Behavior Therapy Skills Workbook: Practical DBT Exercises for Learning Mindfulness, Interpersonal Effectiveness, Emotion Regulation, and Distress Tolerance
by <u>Matthew McKay, Ph.D.</u>, <u>Jeffrey C. Wood, PsyD</u>, and <u>Jeffrey Brantley, MD</u>.

- Self-Esteem: A Proven Program of Cognitive Techniques for Assessing, Improving, and Maintaining Your Self-Esteem
by <u>Matthew McKay, Ph.D.</u>, <u>Patrick Fanning</u>.

Helpful Websites

The following websites are or provide valuable tools for managing teenage anxiety:

- <u>https://locator.apa.org/?partner=nlm</u>: This is the American Psychological Association's psychologist locator.

- <u>https://findtreatment.samhsa.gov/</u>: SAMHSA stands for Substance Abuse and Mental Health Services Administration. This is a behavioral health treatment services locator.

- <u>https://www.nami.org/Your-Journey/Kids-Teens-and-Young-Adults</u>: The National Alliance on Mental Health has a lot of helpful information on managing mental health in college and making friends.

- http://mindfulnessforteens.com/: Mindfulness for Teens teaches kids how to handle stress and reduce anxiety with mindful meditation. It has an accompanying app.

- http://www.headmeds.org.uk/: This website provides information on the most common medicines prescribed for mental health conditions, focusing on the youth.

Anxiety Apps

Breathe2Relax

Have a tough time managing your anxiety level while you're on the go? This app's got you. It is a "portable stress management tool which provides detailed information on the effects of stress on the body and instructions and practice exercises." This app is available for both iOS and Android devices.

Link to the Apple store: https://apps.apple.com/us/app/breathe2relax/id425720246.

Link to the Google Play Store: https://play.google.com/store/apps/details?id=org.t2health.breathe2relax&hl=en&gl=US.

Calm

This app, along with its website (https://www.calm.com), allows you to work on improving your mental health through stress and anxiety reduction techniques but also helps enhance sleep quality and focus. It has many meditation scripts, music, breathing exercises, and more. Some of its content is free, while others are paid. I use Calm daily to meditate and find the content very helpful.

Link to the Apple store: https://apps.apple.com/us/app/calm/id571800810.

Link to the Google Play Store: https://play.google.com/store/apps/details?id=com.calm.android&hl=en&gl=US.

Headspace

Touting itself as the "Most Science-Backed Meditation App," the company has research that shows its methods of mindfulness and meditation have a positive impact on mental and physical health. The app offers a variety of meditations on topics like anxiety, stress, school, and relationships, for example. They also have meditation for beginners. The website link is https://www.headspace.com/.

Link to the Apple store: https://apps.apple.com/us/app/headspace-mindful-meditation/id493145008.

Link to the Google Play Store: https://play.google.com/store/apps/details?id=com.getsomeheadspace.android&hl=enUS&gl=US.

IN THE END...

Occasional bouts of anxiety are a normal part of everyday life. As adults, we worry about the bills, the future, job security, and building success. Plus, relationships and health are added concerns for adults.

These problems often overshadow the worries that plague teenagers, like body image, bullying, schoolwork, maintaining grades, hobbies, athletics, and the pressures to live up to ideals perpetrated in social media. Even though overshadowed, these worries are no less significant. More importantly, they pass with time.

It's when worries turn into a constant state of angst and anxiety that a problem occurs. This is when a teen seems always to be followed by a dark cloud of doom and despair. When these feelings remain intense and excessive, this is a problem.

Human beings have an uncanny ability to solve problems. Look at all that we have invented. If we were not such inventive creatures, we would not have created homes, and caves would still be our preferred dwellings. We might not imitate birds and fly in planes, nor would we glimpse a fish's life from boats.

In the same breath, we would not analyze the anatomy of anxiety and dissect its parts to overcome it. It is within our nature to solve problems, and anxiety is a serious problem. Do you know the default and oh-so-true assumptions derived from this? You have the power to overcome anxiety. You do not have to reinvent the wheel to do it, either. Humans have studied anxiety for a long time. Science has found the tried-and-true ways that work best to gain mastery over your teenager's mind and what goes on in it. This book does not try to reinvent the wheel, either. It gives you those solutions in simple language, along with my personal experiences as a teen with anxiety and a parent who mothers a child with anxiety. Our experiences were written to help you. Use that help liberally, especially in the wake of the COVID-19 crisis, which has caused a sharp spike in teenage anxiety. Understand the types of anxiety that exist and their symptoms. Help your teenager make lifestyle changes like adopting a well-balanced diet, maintaining good sleep hygiene, journaling, and performing self-care. Teach them the arts of deep breathing and meditation. Help them monitor their thoughts and how they affect their actions. Practice cognitive behavioral therapy (CBT) and dialectical behavior therapy (DBT). Be gentle and allow yourself the time and grace to overcome this challenge and not get it right every single time. These and other practices outlined in this book are small acts but are highly effective at taming the effects of anxiety in teenagers.

Am I promising your child will be miraculously cured of anxiety by using them? Of course not. What I am saying is that you can take a proactive approach and *do* something to help them overcome this affliction instead of just accepting the dismal symptoms. I am saying that with consistent effort and noting what works best for them, you can turn their lives into something where you both look forward to waking up in the morning. I am saying that anxiety does not have to control your teenager or your family life any longer. You can take the reins and steer them into happier, more fulfilling times. I am saying that you now have the tools in your arsenal to make that a reality. I implore you to use them. Don't wait. Start today!

While you're at it, help another parent struggling to tame teenage anxiety in their household. If you have found this book helpful, please leave a review of this book on Amazon. It takes a few minutes to do, but the effect is enormous. It helps other families who need help to find it in this book.

Thank you for paying it forward and good luck finally seeing the sunshine on the other side of the dark cloud that is anxiety.

REFERENCES

4 CBT Activities for Teenagers. (2022, July 18). Imagine Bellevue. Retrieved October 20, 2022, from https://www.bellevueimagine.com/mental-health-blog/cbt-activities-for-teenagers/.

4 Differences Between CBT and DBT and How to Tell Which is Right for You. (2019, October 3). Skyland Trail. Retrieved October 19, 2022, from https://www.skylandtrail.org/4-differences-between-cbt-and-dbt-and-how-to-tell-which-is-right-for-you/.

10 Easy Breathing Exercises for Anxiety. (2022, June 16). Verywell Health. Retrieved October 19, 2022, from https://www.verywellhealth.com/breathing-exercises-for-anxiety-5088091.

60 Free Ways to Show Random Acts of Kindness for Teens. (2017, February 13). Informed Decisions. Retrieved October 19, 2022, from https://informeddecisionsblog.com/2017/02/13/60-free-ways-to-show-random-acts-of-kindness-for-teens/.

99 Coping. (n.d.). Retrieved October 19, 2022, from https://www.yourlifeyourvoice.org/journalpages/99-coping-skills-poster.pdf?Topic=Coping+Skills.

About ERP for Pediatric OCD. (2015, July 9). OCD in Kids. Retrieved October 20, 2022, from https://kids.iocdf.org/professionals/mh/about-erp-for-pediatric-ocd/.

About Prolonged Exposure Therapy | Center for the Treatment and Study of Anxiety | Perelman School of Medicine at the University of Pennsylvania. (n.d.). Retrieved October 20, 2022, from https://www.med.upenn.edu/ctsa/workshops_pet.html.

Adherence to Mediterranean diet improves teens' grades. (2018, July 18). Retrieved October 19, 2022, from https://www.healio.com/news/pediatrics/20180718/adherence-to-mediterranean-diet-improves-teens-grades.

Agoraphobia Explained By Analogy Metaphor Examples. (n.d.). Retrieved October 19, 2022, from http://www.metamia.com/analogize.php?q=agoraphobia.

Anxiety. (n.d.). Retrieved October 19, 2022, from https://medlineplus.gov/anxiety.html.

Anxiety Disorders. (n.d.). National Institute of Mental Health (NIMH). Retrieved October 19, 2022, from https://www.nimh.nih.gov/health/topics/anxiety-disorders.

Anxiety Disorders: Types, Causes, Symptoms & Treatments. (n.d.). Cleveland Clinic. Retrieved October 19, 2022, from https://my.clevelandclinic.org/health/diseases/9536-anxiety-disorders.

Anxiety in Teens is Rising: What's Going On? (n.d.). HealthyChildren.org. Retrieved October 19, 2022, from https://www.healthychildren.org/English/health-issues/conditions/emotional-problems/Pages/Anxiety-Disorders.aspx.

Anxiety in Teens is Rising: What's Going On? (n.d.-b). HealthyChildren.org. Retrieved October 19, 2022, from https://www.healthychildren.org/English/health-issues/conditions/emotional-problems/Pages/Anxiety-Disorders.aspx.

Barnhill, J. W. (2022, September 30). *Specific Phobic Disorders*. Merck Manuals Consumer Version. Retrieved October 19, 2022, from https://www.merckmanuals.com/home/mental-health-disorders/anxiety-and-stress-related-disorders/specific-phobic-disorders.

Becker-Haimes, E. C., Okamura, K., Wolk, B., Rubin, R., Evans, A., & Beidasa, R. (2017, June). *Predictors of clinician use of exposure therapy in community mental health settings*. NIH NLM. https://www.ncbi.nlm.nih.gov/pmc/articles/PMC5501186/.

The Biochemistry of Anxiety. (2022, August 24). Retrieved October 19, 2022, from https://www.calmclinic.com/anxiety/biochemistry-of-anxiety.

Birmaher MD, B., Khetarpal MD, S., Cully MEd, M., Brent MD, D., & McKenzie PhD, S. (1995, October). *Screen for Child Anxiety Related Disorders (SCARED)*. Oregon Health and Science University. https://www.ohsu.edu/sites/default/files/2019-06/SCARED-form-Parent-and-Child-version.pdf.

Child Mind Institute. (2021, September 10). *2018 Children's Mental Health Report: Understanding Anxiety in Children and Teens*. Retrieved October 19, 2022, from https://childmind.org/awareness-campaigns/childrens-mental-health-report/2018-childrens-mental-health-report/.

Clarke, S. (2020, October 11). *15 Metaphors For Social Anxiety That Will Help You Explain It*. ProjectEnergise.com. Retrieved October 19, 2022, from https://projectenergise.com/metaphors-for-social-anxiety/.

Cognitive Behavioral Therapy (CBT): Types, Techniques, Uses. (2022, August 10). Verywell Mind. Retrieved October 19, 2022, from https://www.verywellmind.com/what-is-cognitive-behavior-therapy-2795747.

Communication, C. F. P. A. T. (2019, October 16). *The Power of Exercise for Teens*. Center for Parent and Teen Communication. Retrieved October 19, 2022, from https://parentandteen.com/stress-management-teens-exercise/.

Counselor. (2015, July 30). *The anxiety experience: 7 metaphors to illustrate anxiety*. Counselling Directory. https://www.counselling-directory.org.uk/memberarticles/the-anxiety-experience-7-metaphors-to-illustrate-anxiety#:~:text=6.,move%2C%20anxiety%20tightens%20the%20grips.

Dattani, S. (2021, August 20). *Mental Health*. Our World in Data. Retrieved October 19, 2022, from https://ourworldindata.org/mental-health.

Elia, J. (2022a, September 26). *Agoraphobia in Children and Adolescents*. Merck Manuals Professional Edition. Retrieved October 19, 2022, from https://www.merckmanuals.com/professional/pediatrics/mental-disorders-in-children-and-adolescents/agoraphobia-in-children-and-adolescents.

Elia, J. (2022, September 26). *Generalized Anxiety Disorder in Children and Adolescents*. Merck Manuals Professional Edition. Retrieved October 19, 2022, from https://www.merckmanuals.com/professional/pediatrics/mental-disorders-in-children-and-adolescents/generalized-anxiety-disorder-in-children-and-adolescents.

Elia, J. (2022b, September 26). *Obsessive-Compulsive Disorder (OCD) and Related Disorders in Children and Adolescents*. Merck Manuals Professional Edition. Retrieved October 19, 2022, from https://www.merckmanuals.com/professional/pediatrics/mental-disorders-in-children-and-adolescents/obsessive-compulsive-disorder-ocd-and-related-disorders-in-children-and-adolescents.

Elia, J. (2022c, September 26). *Panic Disorder in Children and Adolescents*. Merck Manuals Professional Edition. Retrieved October 19, 2022, from https://www.merckmanuals.com/professional/pediatrics/mental-disorders-in-children-and-adolescents/panic-disorder-in-children-and-adolescents.

Elia, J. (2022d, September 26). *Separation Anxiety Disorder*. Merck Manuals Professional Edition. Retrieved October 19, 2022, from https://www.merckmanuals.com/professional/pediatrics/mental-disorders-in-children-and-adolescents/separation-anxiety-disorder.

Elia, J. (2022b, September 26). *Social Anxiety Disorder in Children and Adolescents*. Merck Manuals Professional Edition. Retrieved October 19, 2022, from https://www.merckmanuals.com/professional/pediatrics/mental-disorders-in-children-and-adolescents/social-anxiety-disorder-in-children-and-adolescents.

Embark Behavioral Health. (2022, July 29). *Sleep Anxiety: What Parents Need To Know*. Retrieved October 19, 2022, from https://www.embarkbh.com/blog/sleep-anxiety-what-parents-need-to-know/.

Explore Teen Suicide in the United States | 2022 Health of Women and Children Report. (n.d.). America's Health Rankings. Retrieved October 21, 2022, from https://www.americashealthrankings.org/explore/health-of-women-and-children/measure/teen_suicide/state/ALL.

Fact Checking Thoughts Worksheet. (2021, March 15). Positive Psychology. https://positive.b-cdn.net/wp-content/uploads/2020/09/Fact-Checking-Thoughts-Worksheet.pdf.

FAQs for Prolonged Exposure (PE) | Center for Deployment Psychology. (n.d.). Retrieved October 20, 2022, from https://deploymentpsych.org/PE-FAQ.

Fenn, K., & Byrne, M. (2013, September 6). *The key principles of cognitive behavioural therapy*. Sage Journals.

https://journals.sagepub.com/doi/full/10.1177/1755738012471029.

Gotter, A. (2019, April 22). *8 Breathing Exercises to Try When You Feel Anxious*. Healthline. Retrieved October 19, 2022, from https://www.healthline.com/health/breathing-exercises-for-anxiety.

Graded Exposure Worksheet. (2020, June 13). Positive Psychology. https://positive.b-cdn.net/wp-content/uploads/Graded-Exposure-Worksheet.pdf.

Harris, A. (2022, June 8). *10 Steps of Radical Acceptance*. DBT Skills | HopeWay. Retrieved October 23, 2022, from https://hopeway.org/blog/radical-acceptance.

How to Manage Anxiety Symptoms After Quitting Drinking Alcohol. (2021, March 1). Retrieved October 19, 2022, from https://www.calmclinic.com/anxiety/types/stopped-drinking.

Jacobson, S. (2022, January 19). *Psychodynamic Psychotherapy vs CBT: Which to Choose?* Harley Therapy™ Blog. Retrieved October 19, 2022, from https://www.harleytherapy.co.uk/counselling/psychodynamic-psychotherapy-vs-cbt.htm.

Karavasilis, C. (2022, October 12). *Cognitive Behavioral Therapy: Benefits for people onboard*. SAFETY4SEA. Retrieved October 19, 2022, from https://safety4sea.com/cm-cognitive-behavioral-therapy-benefits-for-people-onboard/.

Kendall, P., & Peterman, J. (2017, April 10). *CBT for Adolescents With Anxiety: Mature Yet Still Developing.*

Focus: The Journal of Lifelong Learning in Psychiatry. https://focus.psychiatryonline.org/doi/10.1176/appi.focus.15206.

Klein, Y. (2020, February 19). *This One DBT Skill Can Lift Most Teens' Negative Moods*. Evolve Treatment Centers. Retrieved October 20, 2022, from https://evolvetreatment.com/blog/dbt-skill-teens-moods/.

Learn How to Make a Mindfulness Meditation Practice Part of Your Day. (2022, September 22). Verywell Mind. Retrieved October 19, 2022, from https://www.verywellmind.com/mindfulness-meditation-88369.

McMakina, D., & Alfanob, C. (2015, November 28). *Sleep and Anxiety in Late Childhood and Early Adolescence*. NIH NLM. https://www.ncbi.nlm.nih.gov/pmc/articles/PMC4670558/.

Miller, C., Bubrick, J., PhD, & Anderson, D., PhD. (2022, October 11). *How Anxiety Affects Teenagers*. Child Mind Institute. Retrieved October 19, 2022, from https://childmind.org/article/signs-of-anxiety-in-teenagers/.

Miller, C., & Taskiran, S., MD. (2022, July 28). *Mental Health Disorders and Teen Substance Use*. Child Mind Institute. Retrieved October 19, 2022, from https://childmind.org/article/mental-health-disorders-and-substance-use/.

Monroe, J. (2022, October 14). *Yoga for Anxiety and Depression*. Newport Academy. Retrieved October 19, 2022, from https://www.newportacademy.com/resources/well-being/yoga-for-anxiety/.

Murphy, R., Straebler, S., Cooper, Z., & Fairburn, C. (2010, September). *Cognitive Behavioral Therapy for Eating Disorders*. NIH NLM. https://www.ncbi.nlm.nih.gov/pmc/articles/PMC2928448/.

Naidoo, U., MD. (2020, October 27). *Eating well to help manage anxiety: Your questions answered*. Harvard Health. Retrieved October 19, 2022, from https://www.health.harvard.edu/blog/eating-well-to-help-manage-anxiety-your-questions-answered-2018031413460.

Norwitz, N. G. (2021). *Nutrition as Metabolic Treatment for Anxiety*. Frontiers. Retrieved October 19, 2022, from https://www.frontiersin.org/articles/10.3389/fpsyt.2021.598119/full.

nytimes.com. (2020, March 2). Retrieved October 19, 2022, from https://www.nytimes.com/2020/03/02/well/family/the-benefits-of-exercise-for-childrens-mental-health.html.

Picciotto, M., Brunzell, D., & Caldarone, B. (2002, July 2). *Effect of nicotine and nicotinic receptors on anxiety and depression*. NIH NLM. https://pubmed.ncbi.nlm.nih.gov/12151749/.

Poulsen, S., Daniel, S., Lunn, S., Folke, S., Mathiesen, B., Katznelson, H., & Fairburn, C. (n.d.). *A Randomized*

Controlled Trial of Psychoanalytic Psychotherapy or Cognitive-Behavioral Therapy for Bulimia Nervosa. The American Journal of Psychiatry. Retrieved January 1, 2014, from https://ajp.psychiatryonline.org/doi/full/10.1176/appi.ajp.2013.12121511.

Prolonged Exposure (PE). (2017b, May). Clinical Practice Guideline for the Treatment of Posttraumatic Stress Disorder (PTSD). https://www.apa.org/ptsd-guideline/treatments/prolonged-exposure.

Prolonged Exposure Therapy for Adolescents with PTSD. (n.d.). Retrieved October 20, 2022, from https://preventionservices.acf.hhs.gov/programs/279/show.

Psychiatry Online. (n.d.). The American Journal of Psychiatry. Retrieved October 19, 2022, from https://ajp.psychiatryonline.org/action/cookieAbsent.

Rae, S. (2020, May 25). *What is the most visible thing you see in a person with social anxiety?* Quora. https://www.quora.com/What-is-the-most-visible-thing-you-see-in-a-person-with-social-anxiety/answer/Shanez-Rae/log.

Sadeghi, O., Keshteli, A., Afshar, H., Esmaillzadeh, A., & Adibi, P. (2021, April). *Adherence to Mediterranean dietary pattern is inversely associated with depression, anxiety and psychological distress*. NIH NLM. https://pubmed.ncbi.nlm.nih.gov/31185883/#:~:text=When%20the%20association%20with%20components,depression%2C%20anxiety%20and%20psychological%20distress.

Schuster, S. (2020, April 23). *23 Metaphors That Might Help You Explain What a Panic Attack Feels Like*. The Mighty. Retrieved October 19, 2022, from https://themighty.com/topic/panic-disorder/panic-attack-metaphors.

Self-Care Wellness Toolkit. (2015, August). Humboldt State University Student Health & Wellness Services. https://wellbeing.humboldt.edu/sites/default/files/health/Self%20Care%20Wellness%20Toolkit%20for%20Depression%20and%20Anxiety_for%20website.pdf.

Seligman, L., & Ollendick, T. (2012, April 1). *Cognitive Behavioral Therapy for Anxiety Disorders in Youth*. NIH NLM. https://www.ncbi.nlm.nih.gov/pmc/articles/PMC3091167/.

Silva, L. (2022, August 4). *How To Deal With Anxiety*. Forbes Health. Retrieved October 19, 2022, from https://www.forbes.com/health/mind/how-to-deal-with-anxiety/.

Staff, M. (2022, October 4). *How to Meditate with Anxiety*. Mindful. Retrieved October 19, 2022, from https://www.mindful.org/mindfulness-meditation-anxiety/.

Team, S. (2022, June 12). *Anxiety statistics 2022*. The Checkup. Retrieved October 19, 2022, from https://www.singlecare.com/blog/news/anxiety-statistics/.

Team, B. A. S. (2022, March 15). *How to Use Meditation for Teen Stress and Anxiety*. Cleveland Clinic Health

Essentials. Retrieved October 19, 2022, from https://health.clevelandclinic.org/how-to-use-meditation-for-teen-stress-and-anxiety/.

Teenagers and Sleep: How Much Sleep Is Enough? (2022, March 25). Johns Hopkins Medicine. Retrieved October 19, 2022, from https://www.hopkinsmedicine.org/health/wellness-and-prevention/teenagers-and-sleep-how-much-sleep-is-enough.

Therapy, M. (2018, October 25). *8 Areas of Self-Care:* Modern Therapy. Retrieved October 19, 2022, from https://moderntherapy.online/blog-2/areas-of-self-care.

Thomas, F. (2021, July 2). *4 metaphors for anxiety.* Happiful Magazine. Retrieved October 19, 2022, from https://happiful.com/4-metaphors-for-anxiety/.

Thought Record Worksheet. (2021, March 12). Positive Psychology. https://positive.b-cdn.net/wp-content/uploads/2018/01/Thought-Record-Worksheet.pdf.

Walen, A. L. (2018, July 9). *Cortisol and Anxiety Go Hand-In-Hand | Center for Eating Disorders Management, NH.* CEDM. Retrieved October 19, 2022, from https://www.cedm-inc.com/2018/07/09/cortisol-and-anxiety-go-hand-in-hand/.

Wall, D. (2021, June 18). *Anxiety Disorders.* ABCT - Association for Behavioral and Cognitive Therapies. Retrieved October 19, 2022, from https://www.abct.org/fact-sheets/anxiety-disorders/.

What Is Radical Acceptance? (2021, May 26). Verywell Mind. Retrieved October 23, 2022, from https://www.verywellmind.com/what-is-radical-acceptance-5120614.

What is your favorite analogy for OCD? (2013, November 10). Reddit. Retrieved October 19, 2022, from https://www.reddit.com/r/OCD/comments/1qbhnl/what_is_your_favorite_analogy_for_ocd/.

Which Types of Therapy Are Best for Teens? (2022, February 25). Verywell Mind. Retrieved October 19, 2022, from https://www.verywellmind.com/therapy-for-teens-2610410.

Whyte, A. (2021, November 29). *How Adolescent DBT Programs Help Depressed and Anxious Teens*. Evolve Treatment Centers. Retrieved October 19, 2022, from https://evolvetreatment.com/blog/dbt-depressed-anxious-teens/.

Whyte, A. (2021a, June 15). *Teen Stress and Anxiety: Facts and Statistics*. Evolve Treatment Centers. Retrieved October 19, 2022, from https://evolvetreatment.com/blog/teen-stress-anxiety-facts/.

Made in the USA
Monee, IL
17 September 2024

66013681R00125